On Synthesizing
Marxism and Christianity

ON SYNTHESIZING
MARXISM AND CHRISTIANITY

DALE VREE

WITHDRAWN

A WILEY-INTERSCIENCE PUBLICATION

JOHN WILEY & SONS, New York · London · Sydney · Toronto

Library of Congress Cataloging in Publication Data

Vree, Dale, 1944-
    On Synthesizing Marxism and Christianity.

"A Wiley-Interscience publication."
Bibliography: p.
1. Communism and Christianity. I. Title.

HX536.V74   261.7   76-27706
ISBN 0-471-01603-9

Printed in the United States of America

10 9 8 7 6 5 4 3 2 1

To my father
Henry Vree
a dear man
a profound influence

Preface

The Marxist-Christian dialogue has quickly proceeded beyond the stage of mutual curiosity and polite conversation to the stage of spirited solidarity and intellectual convergence. Published writings and public conferences on the dialogue have been generally supportive of various efforts to synthesize Marxism and Christianity, that is, to either Christify Marxism or communize Christianity. Much of the sympathy for these efforts is built on the attractive premise that in a world which could destroy itself at any time, harmonious or convergent dialogue between Marxism (often equated with the East) and Christianity (often equated with the West) is a moral imperative. It is not my intention to deny or affirm this premise or valuation. Instead, I will put it off to the side and probe a more difficult issue, namely, whether what is desired here is commensurate with what is possible. Is synthesis allowable given the basic character of Marxism and Christianity?

The subject of synthetic Marxist-Christian dialogue has been highly controversial. But although much of the literature and discussion has been provocative, amid all the partisanship what has not been written—but should have been written long ago—

is a work that dispassionately analyzes the dialogue from a neutral frame of reference, that clearly delineates the high intellectual stakes involved in Marxist-Christian synthesis. I have taken my task to be the writing of just such a work. As such, this book is designed to be a novel and original contribution to the Marxist-Christian dialogue.

The thesis I shall advance is that Marxism and Christianity are disjunctive belief systems, that synthetic dialogue between the two is destructive of both basic Marxism and traditional Christianity, and that hybrid world views are incompatible with parent world views. It may be preferable that Marxism and Christianity destroy themselves rather than hasten the destruction of the world (in their attempts to guard their mutual identities); however, this is a judgment I shall not presume to make. Lest the reader consider this whole procedure nihilistic or value-free, let him or her be reminded that the quest for intellectual clarity is itself a moral imperative.

It is only fair to add—in a study such as this which attempts to be dispassionate and reasonably objective—that I do have my own personal commitments. Although I demonstrate why Christianity and Marxism are incompatible, I do not come to this conclusion to aid the forces of privilege, reaction, cold war, or hot war. It is not my intention to argue that Christians and Marxists should not talk to one another. Nor is it my intention to argue that Christians cannot be socialists. For indeed, I count myself as both a (generally orthodox) Christian and a (rather eclectic) socialist—although I make no claims for the truth of Christianity or the desirability of any kind of socialism in this book. I would even say that a Christian can be a Marxist, as long as he or she does not buy the whole package. Elements of Marxism that a Christian cannot accept are discussed in this book.

The question of the compatibility of Marxism and Christianity is not merely an academic one for me. I have struggled personally with it for the last fifteen years—that is, all my adult life and part of my adolescence. And let me add that the conclusion I come to here is not the conclusion with which I began my search.

I am of the conviction that anyone can write a book advocating Christian-Marxism (or Christian anti-Marxism). However, such books are usually subjective statements, disguised intellectual autobiographies. Rarely do such books tell us anything about the character of Marxism and Christianity as systems of thought and action, which is precisely what we need to know about. We do not need to know what Professor Q or the Reverend K likes or dislikes about Marxism or Christianity. Such testimonials do little to advance our understanding of the fundamental issues involved in synthetic dialogue. What we need to know about is what Marxism and Christianity are as belief systems, what they claim for themselves. Only then can meaningful Marxist-Christian dialogue take place. Otherwise, all we are likely to get is esoteric conversation between idiosyncratic individuals. Such talk is usually interesting, but it has little impact on official institutions in the real world—churches, parties, and even governments—which will perhaps have something to say about East-West relations, and the survival of the world as we know it.

But to talk about Marxism and Christianity as belief systems, we must put to the side our prejudices, moral commitments, and metaphysical presuppositions. To do this, I have found the employment of certain tools borrowed from the tradition of analytic philosophy to be highly profitable. (Nevertheless, as is the case with almost any work of social theory, I have been forced to make many intellectual judgments and interpretations that are anything but strictly logico-empirical, anything but invincible and closed to disputation.) I know that, despite my best efforts to be unbiased, the thesis advanced herein is controversial. I look forward to the criticisms and rejoinders which, inevitably, will be vociferous.

Belief systems are not physical sense objects. That, however, does not mean they cannot be treated empirically or intersubjectively. A stone is a fact, but so is the existence of a particular belief system. The former is a physical fact, the latter a social fact. A statement about a stone may be factual, just as a statement about a particular belief system may be. The assertion that "these Marxists believe X" may be verifiable, although "X" itself may not be a fact at all nor even be amenable to verification or falsification procedures.

I shall make no substantive claims about the truth or falsity of "X." I shall not make any judgments about the truth or falsity of Marxism or Christianity, or about which varieties are true or false. I shall try to avoid all exegetical disputes concerning what Marx or Jesus or St. Paul "really" meant when they said this or that. Rather, I shall treat Marxism and Christianity as social facts, as the conceptual systems which they are. This means I shall analyze their intellectual structures, ascertain their root presuppositions and internal language norms, and determine what it makes sense to say within these given linguistic contexts. I shall map out the linguistic frontiers of normal or paradigmatic Marxist and Christian discourse, distinguishing such discourse respectively from non-Marxist and non-Christian discourse. As for those arguments employed to promote Marxist-Christian synthesis, I shall scrutinize their logical consistency, measure their fidelity to traditions of Marxist and Christian discourse, and spell out their implications for Marxism and Christianity as systems of thought and action. As such, this work is written in the tradition of ordinary language philosophy by one who is seeking to apply some of the insights of Ludwig Wittgenstein.[1]

For the purposes of this exercise, I am determined, with the "later" Wittgenstein, to avoid the urge to legislate what may pass for cognitive or truthful communication. I intend to respect the actual usages of Marxist and Christian discourse, to note the logic of those usages, and therefore to leave things as they are, so to speak. This does not mean that I am personally indifferent to the truth claims of Marxism and Christianity; it is simply that I am not addressing myself to those issues here. Nor does this mean that I am beholden to some bias in favor of stasis, that I am hostile to intellectual innovation. Wittgenstein himself granted that linguistic contexts (or "forms of life") grow and that linguistic boundaries are fluid. Nevertheless, he insisted that there *are* boundaries. It is this Wittgensteinian contention that I shall seek to substantiate. At issue therefore is whether syntheses of Marxism and Christianity violate the linguistic boundaries of the living linguistic traditions known as Marxism and Christianity.

It is not my assumption that Marxism and Christianity are dead belief systems, incapable of change, or carved in granite once and for all. As is discussed below, both Marxism and Christianity allow for *doctrinal development;* however, there are certain standards at work within both belief systems by which *development* may and must be distinguished from *degeneration* (that is, "illegitimate" doctrinal development).

To be quite specific, I conceive my task to be that of conceptual analysis. In common with others who take this approach, I hope that the result will be therapeutic, that "mental cramps" will be cured and conceptual befuddlement dispelled.

To analyze conceptually any proposed Marxist-Christian hybrid, it is imperative to understand exactly what Marxism and Christianity claim for themselves. There are and have been many versions of Marxism and Christianity. This is an initial problem. Unless we can make pertinent distinctions between these versions, we cannot begin to gain a conceptual and interpretive foothold on the dialogical phenomenon. I shall not, however, try to decide which versions are true. All I shall do, because it must be done in order to proceed, is to decide which versions are normative or paradigmatic. Given my neutral frame of reference, I shall take *normative Christianity* to be whatever most Christians, most of the time, have believed. *Normative Marxism* I shall take to be whatever most Marxists, most of the time, have believed. There is no other way to get at the concept of normativeness without engaging in polemical argumentation as to which versions are true or false.

The most fruitful distinctions to be made are between *orthodoxy* and *heresy* (or heterodoxy) in the case of Christianity and between *official ideology* and *revisionism* in the case of Marxism. It is these distinctions that yield the greatest insight into what is at stake in synthetic dialogue. Orthodoxy or officiality are simply *the marks of authority that are earned by habitual and consensual usage; they are the standards or internal norms that historically come to govern what may "legitimately" be said within the linguistic contexts* known as Christianity and Marxism, respectively.

Although the identification of heresy is not especially popular now in the Christian world, throughout its history the church has taken great pains to define, identify, and root out heresy. Inasmuch as current dialogical modes of thought more or less duplicate certain well-known heresies, it is still possible to utilize the concept of heresy efficaciously.

The term that best explains what is meant by official Marxism is *partiinost* (Russian for "Party-mindedness"), according to which truth is whatever the Communist Party says it is. Soviet Marxism is the dominant form of Marxism in the world today. Within the European and North American area (which is the chief context of the intellectual form of the dialogue) the Soviet Party is always taken to represent the standard of orthodox Marxism, which usually goes by the name of Marxism-Leninism.

The use of these concepts (orthodox and heretical, official and revisionist) is symmetrical since, in the words of Leopold Labedz, "revisionism is to Marxist movements what heresy is to religious ones. . . . Heresy is the shadow of every orthodoxy, and Marxism is no exception."[2] However, it must not be forgotten that heresy and revisionism originate from within the given belief system, not from without. Hence, to define heresy and revisionism is a delicate matter. Heresy is not apostasy or blatant unbelief; revisionism is not outright counterrevolution. Yet, because heresy takes up residence within the household of faith itself, because revisionism takes hold within the very citadel of "truth," they are potentially more beguiling and threatening than apostasy and counterrevolution, because more difficult to discern.

I do not use "heretic" and "revisionist" as scare words. Likewise, "orthodox" and "official" are not intended to be pejoratives. It is merely that these words have achieved a certain status by virtue of their regular usage and wide application in ordinary language. We may not like these labels but it cannot be denied that they are useful landmarks for piecing together a cognitive map that will facilitate conceptual analysis. These terms have such universal recognition that even accused heretics uphold them. As a rule, they either turn around and accuse the orthodox of being the *real* heretics or they glory in their heretical posture (noting perhaps that Socrates and Jesus were something of "heretics" in their own day). For Marxists or Christians to declare that the categories of heresy and revisionism are in principle irrelevant is tantamount to declaring that the discrimination of truth from error does not interest them. Such declarations are, of course, intellectually self-defeating.

What I shall do is use these concepts in a clinical sense and thereby establish the fact that there *is* a Christian orthodoxy, that there *is* a Marxist orthodoxy. I shall deal with Christian orthodoxy in terms of: (1) the source and nature of revelation, (2) Original Sin, and (3) the Kingdom of God. I shall deal with Marxist orthodoxy in terms of: (1) the character of its atheism, (2) the nature of its determinism and the controversy surrounding the young Marx, and (3) the role of the Party. Hence, I shall not be constructing an inventory of all possible heresies and deviations; rather, I shall limit myself to these particular stipulated issues.

Beyond that, I shall show that, regardless of the merits of their claims to truth, these orthodoxies are conceptually significant because they manifest a logic, there is a point to them, and, indeed, they make a certain kind of sense. As such, I shall show that these orthodoxies are not necessarily arbitrary and capricious; hence, to tamper with their integral consistency is not only a violation of linguistic frontiers, but a grave matter for those who claim to speak in the name of Marxism or Christianity. Finally, I shall show how dialogical Christians and dialogical Marxists, in departing from their respective orthodoxies, place more weight on the concept of human freedom than their respective belief systems can sustain, and hence fall into philosophical confusion.

The available literature on the international Marxist-Christian dialogue is so diverse and extensive that a complete discussion of the subject is probably beyond the capacity of any one writer—and would unduly tax the patience of even the most diligent reader. This is especially true when one considers that prerequisite to dealing with this literature is a thorough knowledge of the history of both Christianity and Marxism, as well as a familiarity with the political, philosophical, and theological currents in numerous countries. Therefore, I have decided to focus on the most intellectually challenging aspect of the dialogue, namely, *synthetic* dialogue. Moreover, I make no pretense that my study of synthetic dialogue is comprehensive or exhaustive. Rather, I have designed it to be selective and representative.[3]

I have, therefore, chosen two Christians and one Marxist for special treatment. All three have been pacesetters in the unfolding dialogue and are representative of what synthetic dialogue entails. The Marxist is Roger Garaudy. The Christians are Harvey Cox and Juergen Moltmann. All three have been ongoing participants in the synthetic dialogue rather than episodic contributors (such as Ernst Bloch, Wolfhart Pannenberg, or Leslie Dewart).

Synthetic dialogue has assumed practical political importance in Czechoslovakia (before the Soviet invasion in 1968) and in France (prior to the eclipse of organized Christian Democracy in the late 1960s). Although its intellectual influence lingers in France, its practical political importance has not diminished in Italy (where, despite Vatican misgivings, the Christian Democrats and the Communists have been slowly moving toward a political alliance) or in Yugoslavia (where the interaction of Christians and Communists has been more complex and less dramatic than in Italy). The political importance of synthetic dialogue can be expected to increase in Spain (where the groundwork for Catholic-Communist collaboration has long since been established in the quasi-clandestine trade union movement, and even by some leaders of the Church and leaders of the Communist apparatus).

But nowhere has its importance been greater than in Latin America, where dialogical Catholicism is now known as "liberation theology." Here Marxist-Christian fusion has at times assumed violent revolutionary character (most notably in the case of the martyred guerrilla priest, Camilo Torres), as well as more pacific forms (as in Chile under the Frei and Allende presidencies). One cannot fully appreciate liberation theology without understanding its roots in the thought of Cox and Moltmann—roots this book explores.

I would like to express my deep appreciation to the following people who read all or part of this book in manuscript form,

and offered wise counsel, valuable criticism, and/or needed encouragement: Hugh Barbour, Thomas G. Barnes, Peter L. Berger,
Landrum Bolling, J. M. Cameron, Jyotirindra Das Gupta, Richard
Davis, Joe E. Elmore, Robert E. Fitch, A. James Gregor, Eric Hof-
fer, Irving Kristol, Thomas Molnar, Fr. Robert S. Morse, Paul
Ramsey, Max L. Stackhouse, Stephen J. Tonsor, D. Elton True-
blood, Ernest van den Haag, Eric Voegelin, and Charles C. West.

A special debt of thanks is owed to Paul Seabury, who read
the manuscript more than once, who was always available to
give needed advice (regardless of what part of the world he
happened to be in at a given moment), and whose enthusiasm
for this manuscript was surely equal to the enthusiasm he
shows for his own work. Would that every young scholar were
so fortunate! Needless to say, responsibility for the shortcom-
ings of this book is mine alone.

The writing of this book was facilitated by a summer grant
from the Center for Slavic and East European Studies of the
University of California at Berkeley, a summer Humanities Fa-
culty Development grant from Earlham College, and a two-year
grant from the National Science Foundation.

My parents have witnessed—and endured—my wrestlings
with Marxism and Christianity. I thank them for all their patience and encouragement. They have contributed more than
even they realize.

My wife, Elena, has been a partner in this enterprise in every
sense. Her assistance—running the gamut from the editorial to
the conjugal, the intellectual to the spiritual —has been beyond
calculation, for indeed my struggle with Marxism and Christianity has been her struggle as well. We were, or so it seems,
born involved in one another.

DALE VREE

Institute of International Studies
University of California at Berkeley
June 1976

NOTES

1. For background, see Dale Vree, "Reflections on Wittgenstein, Religion, and Politics," Christian Scholar's Review, III, No. 2 (1973), pp. 113–133.
2. Leopold Labedz, "Introduction," Revisionism, Leopold Labedz, ed. (New York: Praeger, 1962), p. 9.
3. In keeping with this selectivity, I have generally stressed sources available in English. This strategy appeared to be entirely reasonable inasmuch as virtually all the pertinent foreign language literature has been translated. The dialogue has enjoyed a high "relevance quotient" with a segment of the reading public, which publishers have been quick to appreciate. An interesting case is that of James E. Will, who went to Europe in 1968 to seek out literature on the dialogue. Of his experience he wrote: "I returned from sabbatical study . . . to be surprised by the amount of publication becoming available in English in this country. One would hardly have needed to go away!" And that was back in 1968! See James E. Will, "The Uses of Philosophical Theology in the Christian-Marxist Dialogue," Union Seminary Quarterly Review, XXVI (Fall 1970), p. 22n.

Contents

Abbreviations

AD   R. Garaudy, *From Anathema to Dialogue* (New York: Vintage, 1966).

CC   R. Garaudy, *The Crisis in Communism* (New York: Grove, 1970).

CG   J. Moltmann, *The Crucified God* (New York: Harper & Row, 1974).

EH   J. Moltmann, *The Experiment Hope* (Philadelphia: Fortress, 1975) (essays).

FF   H. Cox, *The Feast of Fools* (New York: Harper & Row, 1969).

FH   Frederick Herzog, ed., *The Future of Hope* (New York: Herder and Herder, 1970).

GR   H. Cox, *God's Revolution and Man's Responsibility* (Valley Forge, Pa.: Judson, 1965).

HP   J. Moltmann, *Hope and Planning* (New York: Harper & Row, 1971) (essays).

IH   R. Garaudy, et al., "Initiative in History: A Christian-Marxist Exchange" (pamphlet) (Cambridge, Mass.: The Church Society for College Work, 1967).

MTC   R. Garaudy, *Marxism in the Twentieth Century* (New York: Scribner's, 1970).

NEB   *The New English Bible.*

ON   H. Cox, *On Not Leaving It to the Snake* (New York: Macmillan, 1967) (essays).

RRF   J. Moltmann, *Religion, Revolution and the Future* (New York: Scribner's, 1969) (essays).

SC   H. Cox, *The Secular City,* rev. ed. (New York: Macmillan, 1966).

SCD   Daniel Callahan, ed., *The Secular City Debate* (New York: Macmillan, 1966).

SS   H. Cox, *The Seduction of the Spirit* (New York: Simon and Schuster, 1973).

TCC   *The Christian Century* (Protestant weekly, Chicago).

TH   J. Moltmann, *Theology of Hope* (New York: Harper & Row, 1967).

On Synthesizing
Marxism and Christianity

1

Marxist-Christian Dialogue

> Heresy is the lifeblood of religions. There are
> no heresies in a dead religion.
>
> ANDRÉ SUARÈS

Before proceeding with the conceptual analysis, some prelimi-
nary observations about the historical and psychological setting
of the Marxist-Christian dialogue, as well as some interpretations of its significance, are in order.

The current Marxist-Christian dialogue is characteristic of the
openness of our time. What would have been regarded as suspect or indecent in the West during the 1950s is now granted
respectability—to the point of becoming *de rigueur* in certain
intellectual circles. This transvaluation reflects changes that
have been taking place within the Christian and Communist
worlds, which, in turn, reflect changes that have been occurring
in the world at large. The dialogue can be dated from the papa-

cy of John XXIII and the Second Vatican Council in the Catholic sphere, and the Twentieth Party Congress of the Soviet Communist Party and de-Stalinization in the Communist sphere.

Before the Second Vatican Council, it was common to refer to Roman Catholicism as triumphalist and monolithic. Since the Council, one hears about the crisis in Catholicism—a crisis of authority, credibility, and faith itself. The crisis has been marked by defiance of the teaching authority of the church, defections from holy orders, and a decreasing number of converts. Similarly, during the Stalin era, it was conventional to refer to Communism as aggressive and monolithic. Since de-Stalinization, one hears of polycentrism, which is a polite locution for the crisis that plagues the world Communist movement—a crisis (again) of authority, credibility, and faith. This crisis has been marked by the Soviet invasions of Hungary in 1956 and Czechoslovakia in 1968, the upsurge of revisionism in Eastern and Western Europe, and the Soviet-Chinese schism. The Protestant realm has never been known for its monolithism; however, since the rupture in the neo-orthodox consensus among non-evangelical and nonfundamentalist Protestant theologians within the last fifteen years, everything has become possible, from the formulation of a God-is-dead theology to the endorsement of revolutionary violence and homosexual marriages.

Both the Vatican Council and de-Stalinization grew out of generous impulses and desires for liberalization. However, at a more fundamental level they reflected a crisis of certainty and confidence. What were attempts to set one's own house in order ironically intensified the disorder. What were attempts to establish credibility produced more doubt and incited paroxysms of self-doubt. It was said that all Pope John intended to do was open a window to let some fresh air into the Vatican. Instead, he let in a violent storm. James Hitchcock captured the bitter irony of Catholic reform in these words:

In the heady days of the Council it was common to hear predictions that the conciliar reforms would lead to a massive resurgence of the flagging Catholic spirit. Laymen would be stirred from their apathy and alienation and would join enthusiastically in apostolic projects. Liturgy and theology, having been brought to life and made relevant, would be constant sources of inspiration to the faithful. The religious orders, reformed to bring them into line with modernity, would find themselves overwhelmed with candidates who were generous and enthusiastic. The Church would find the number of converts increasing dramatically as it cast off its moribund visage and indeed would come to be respected and influential in worldly circles as it had not been for centuries. In virtually every case the precise opposite of these predictions has come to pass.[1]

It was said that Khrushchev merely wanted to wash out his dirty linen. Instead, he rent the garment of world Communist unity and very nearly unraveled the fabric of Marxist-Leninist ideology. According to Hans J. Morgenthau, when Khrushchev exposed Stalin in 1956 as a corrupter of Marxism-Leninism, he "cast doubt upon the legitimacy of any ruler or regime governing in the name of Marxism-Leninism." For Morgenthau, the result of liberalization has been that the Soviet government "has lost the moral conviction of its own legitimacy which could overcome the new moral conviction of the dissenters in its midst."[2] What were ventures in revitalization and purification rudely produced degeneration and confusion.

Despite the best efforts of the Vatican and the Kremlin to sustain their claims to infallibility, both Catholicism and Marxism-Leninism have been doctrinally in flux. Significantly, this doctrinal insecurity is regarded by many as a precondition for genuine dialogue, for as Fr. Urban T. Holmes has said, "Clearly whenever anyone agrees to a dialogue he is assuming that there is something in the position of the other than can be of benefit to him and that his own presuppositions are to some extent negotiable."[3] Nevertheless, not all dialogue is genuine dialogue. Some participants in dialogue are less interested in give and take than in capitulation; others are really interested in conversion.

It is not necessary to define what "genuine" dialogue is. Suffice it to say that although dialogue can be an excellent way to strengthen one's own belief system, make it attractive to the outsider, and perhaps co-opt the outsider, certain approaches to dialogue cannot possibly induce a dynamic revitalization of one's own belief system. Here dialogue and self-doubt feed on each other. Here dialogue is a sign of senescence, a prelude to giving up the ghost, or at least a sign of a desire to buy into someone else's belief system. For example, many radical Christians are of the opinion that the church must listen to the "modern world" or "modern man," but not say or proclaim anything to them. An oft-heard slogan is: "The world must set the agenda for the church" (where "the world" is often understood to be a rough euphemism for Marxism). To enter into a dialogue on these terms is to enter into something other than a genuine dialogue. As Peter Berger has said, "'Dialogue' is very often a misleading term. . . . In many cases, it would be more apt to speak of 'conversion' (and I need hardly add that I *don't* mean anybody's conversion to Christianity)."[4] The synthetic dialogue engaged in by Cox and Moltmann is generally of this kind (perhaps "synthetic dialogue" is something of a contradiction in terms). The "dialogue with the modern world" inaugurated by the Vatican Council has at times tended in this direction. Although Christians are more prone to this style of dialogue than Marxists, *mutatis mutandis,* there are Marxists—Garaudy, for example—whose engagement in dialogue has been a prelude to a surrender of their belief system.

Indeed, Dean M. Kelley, in his study on why doctrinally conservative churches are growing, whereas doctrinally lax churches are declining, found the dialogical stance to be a sign of senescence. Kelley, a minister in one of the latitudinarian churches and an official of the broad-minded National Council of Churches, has been an advocate of dialogue between Christians and non-Christians for years. Yet, he warns that those Christians who eschew dialogue "are those whose religious groups are growing, while those who engage in it are the ones whose religious organizations are shrinking."[5] Kelley finds that the spiritually vital churches are those that have not been interested in adjusting to the times and in being on good terms with outsiders, those that have been unafraid to discipline members and take action against alleged heretics.

Why are the tolerant churches declining while the intransigent churches are not? Probably because members of the latter believe they possess a superior and incomparable "truth" of immeasurable worth. As such, they are willing to live for it, sacrifice for it, and proselytise for it. Why have we seen the rise of a Marxist-Christian dialogue? One reason may be because there are fewer Christians and Marxists who are so convinced of the truth and integrity of their received doctrines that they are willing to live unreservedly for that truth and that integrity. This, I suspect, is in part what the Vatican Council and (to a lesser extent) de-Stalinization signify.

This is not to say that intolerance is a virtue, that intolerance itself produces vitality; it is simply to say that intolerance may be symptomatic of vitality. Conversely, certain approaches to dialogue may be symptomatic of senescence. As for senescence, it is important to point out that, on the whole, Christians have shown far greater enthusiasm for the dialogue than Marxists. Prominent Christians engaged in dialogue outnumber prominent Marxists, according to my informal estimates, by three- or four-to-one. Christians frequently articulate the importance of the dialogue in terms of self-preservation and adaptation to the trend of the future, whereas Christianity does not present Marxists with a question of survival. After all, the trend of the last hundred years has been toward the de-Christianization of Christendom and the establishment of Marxism on a world scale. It is the Marxists who enter dialogue from a "world-historical" position of strength.

Those who treat the dialogue as a means of co-optation are more likely to be Marxists than Christians. It is Christians who seem to be more willing to make large sacrifices for the sake of dialogue. Some Christians go so far as to make a wholesale adoption of Marxism (including materialism and even atheism), whereas no Marxist will make a wholesale adoption of traditional Christianity and still call himself a Marxist. It would seem that presently Marxism is a more exclusivist—because more dynamic?—world view than Christianity.

Furthermore, the Vatican, though not indifferent to its doctrine, is more tolerant of dialogue-makers within its fold than most Communist parties are of dialogue-makers within their midst. (Tolerance is unqualified among most Protestants.) For example, in 1969 the Vatican chose not to press formal charges of heresy against Leslie Dewart, a leading dialogical Catholic whose controversial book, *The Future of Belief,* had denied God's personality, his trinitarian nature, and his supernatural existence (though not his "reality"). John Macquarrie, a rather liberal Anglican theologian, found the book to be heretical (Pelagian).[6] The Vatican merely asked Dewart to withhold future editions (which he apparently has not done). Dewart's is not a unique case: since the Council, there have been no heresy trials at all. On the other hand, in 1970 the French Communist Party expelled its chief theoretician, Roger Garaudy, from the Politburo (on which he served for fourteen years) and the Party itself (of which he was a member for more than thirty years). His offense was revisionism—including, in the background, his pioneering role in the dialogue.

Hence, Christians are more serious and enthusiastic about the dialogue than Marxists, and institutional Christianity is on the whole more indulgent toward the dialogue and dialogists than is institutional Marxism. If senescence may be measured by the intensity of an inclination to engage in dialogue, then Christianity (excluding the intolerant variety) would seem to be more senescent than Marxism.

The dialogue is an epiphenomenon of a changing world, of improved relations between East and West. Guenther Nenning suggests that the dialogue represents "a change of ideas following a change of reality." The détente between East and West has "brought about a correspondingly different climate in intellectual superstructure."[7] The old, rigid dichotomies of cold war vintage, such as "Christian anti-Communism" versus "godless Communism," have dissipated. No more do leaders of Western nations threaten a crusade against "atheistic Communism" in the name of and defense of the "Christian West." The appeal to religion has been dropped. The groundwork for a *rapprochement* between Marxism and Christianity was prepared by the growing reality of détente.

To be sure, the very existence of a Christian West has been thrown into doubt by the accelerated pace of secularization and de-Christianization in Western Europe and North America. There is a curious coincidence between secularization since the late 1950s and abatement of the cold war since the same period. One explanation of this coincidence may be that the decline of religion has weakened one of the most salient motives for hostility to Communism.[8]

It is generally recognized that the will of Americans to fight Communism is now at an all-time low. The decline of religion may have had something to do with this. It cannot be gainsaid that to defend God, religion, and one's coreligionists is a powerful motive for wanting to resist Communism—which has a reputation for hostility to religion. Few people, however, have expressed a desire to fight for capitalism. Democracy is more frequently invoked, but democracy is more a procedural than a substantive objective. Furthermore, democracy may not be appropriate for every society or culture. As such, democracy has limited emotional salience. Patriotism would seem to be a stronger motive for combat; however, there is no necessary connection between patriotism and a willingness to "save" other nations from Communism. Patriotism is generally activated when the enemy is on one's very doorstep—and then it may be too late. To put the matter in Marxist language: since ruling classes and imperialist nations have always used religion to protect their interests, to detach religion and religious loyalties from those classes and nations is to deprive them of one of their classical ideological defenses.

Hence, international stabilization and secularization have played havoc with the coherence of the rationale of Western societies. As Morgenthau has observed, "the Soviet bloc in Europe, with the minor exception of Rumania, remains as coherent as it has always been, and the Kremlin is resolved to keep it that way. It is in the West that disintegration is the order of the day. . . ."[9] This incoherence was reflected in the oft-expressed bewilderment with the purposes of the anti-Communist war in Indochina. Why, Americans and Europeans frequently asked, is it so important to prevent the spread of Communism there?

If the Marxist-Christian dialogue is a product of international stabilization and secularization, the dialogue in turn reinforces and legitimizes the East-West détente. However, it actually takes this development one step further. Since Christian intellectuals enter into dialogue without an obligatory Christian political philosophy to defend, they easily slip into a discussion of political matters which is determined by Marxist categories. Furthermore, Marxists, by the very nature of their belief system, do not seem tempted by traditional theism, whereas Christians, by the very nature of their heritage, do seem tempted by what they see as an earthly avenue to the New Jerusalem. As a result, the dialogue tends to draw Christians away from a loyalty to "capitalist democracy" and toward an affinity with Marxist political ideas. The cause of Communism is strengthened while anti-Communism is weakened.

But as much as Communism stands to gain from the dialogue, it will be shown below that the dialogue presents the Marxist-Leninist movement with certain risks and hazards it may not be willing to entertain.

Now let us proceed to the conceptual analysis.

NOTES

1. James Hitchcock, *The Decline and Fall of Radical Catholicism* (New York: Herder and Herder, 1971), p. 24.
2. Hans J. Morgenthau, "Thoughts on the October Revolution: The Political Cost," *The New Leader, L* (November 6, 1967), pp. 14, 15. Also see Hannah Arendt, *The Origins of Totalitarianism,* new ed. (New York: Harcourt Brace Jovanovich, 1973), p. xxix.
3. Urban T. Holmes, "Christian-Marxist Dialogue: The Future of Hope," *The Living Church, 161* (November 22, 1970), p. 13.
4. Peter L. Berger, "A Call for Authority in the Christian Community," *The Princeton Seminary Bulletin, 64* (December 1971), p. 19. The notion that the world must set the agenda for the church was expressed by the dialogical Catholic, Leslie Dewart, in these words: "We do not want the world to embrace the Church; we want the Church to embrace the world" [L. Dewart, "Christians and Marxians in Dialogue," *Continuum, I* (Summer 1963), p. 143]. This idea that the world must set the agenda for the church was attacked (along with other "false and debilitating" notions) by a group of prominent, *non*fundamentalist church people who drafted the so-called Hartford Appeal. Among the twenty-five signers were Peter L. Berger, William Sloane Coffin, Jr., Fr. Avery Dulles, George W. Forell, Stanley Hauerwas, George A. Lindbeck, Richard J. Mouw, Richard

John Neuhaus, Fr. Alexander Schmemann, Nathan A. Scott, Jr., Lewis B. Smedes, Fr. George H. Tavard, and Fr. Bruce Vawter. See "An Appeal for Theological Affirmation," *Worldview,* 18 (April 1975), pp. 39–41.

5. Dean M. Kelley, *Why Conservative Churches Are Growing* (New York: Harper & Row, 1972), p. 160. Cf. Reginald W. Bibby and Merlin B. Brinkerhoff, "The Circulation of the Saints: A Study of People Who Join Conservative Churches," *Journal for the Scientific Study of Religion,* 12 (September 1973), pp. 273–283.

6. John Macquarrie, review of *The Future of Belief* by Leslie Dewart, *Union Seminary Quarterly Review, XXII* (March 1967), p. 261.

7. Guenther Nenning, "In Place of an Introduction," *Dialogue* (Vienna), (Spring 1968), p. 3.

8. For data that tend to support this hypothesis, see Samuel A. Stouffer, *Communism, Conformity, and Civil Liberties* (New York: Wiley, 1955), pp. 165–166, 169.

9. Hans J. Morgenthau, "Superpower Politics: After the Summit," *The New Leader, LV* (June 26, 1972), p. 12.

2
Toward Understanding Dialogical Christianity

The Church is the only thing that saves us from the
degrading slavery of becoming children of our times.

G. K. CHESTERTON

THE SIGNIFICANCE AND IDENTITY OF ORTHODOXY AND HERESY

As indicated in the Preface we are proceeding on the (quite
secular) assumption that orthodox Christianity is *normative*
Christianity, which in turn is what most Christians, most of the
time, have believed. It is remarkable how this assumption harmonizes with one of the classical definitions of traditional orthodoxy. Orthodoxy, said St. Vincent of Lérins in 434, is *quod
ubique, quod semper, quod ab omnibus creditum est* (that
which has been believed everywhere, ever, by everyone).[1]

It goes without saying that Christians believe in the Bible;

however, the Scriptures lend themselves to a multitude of doctrinal interpretations. Their meaning is not transparent. For example, Christians are said to believe in the Incarnation of Christ and the Holy Trinity; but although it certainly implies these doctrines, the New Testament does not even mention these terms. It was the Church, through its *tradition,* which claimed to speak authoritatively on these doctrinal matters. The doctrines of tradition were codified at Ecumenical Councils. There were seven such Councils in the ecumenical or so-called "undivided Church" (i.e., the Church antecedent to the great schism of ca. 1054). As responses to perceived heresies and de facto divisions within the Church, it was these Councils (the last one taking place in 787) which, by expelling heretics, gave expression to what was believed "everywhere, ever, by everyone."

But why was the tradition of the Church regarded as the authoritative interpreter of the Scriptures? Because the Church believed that the Holy Spirit inspired the tradition of the Church. Christians have always believed the Scriptures to be inspired by the Holy Spirit. However, the Scriptures did not fall out of the heavens whole. Before there was such a thing as canonical Scripture there was the Church. It was the Church that had to decide which of the candidate books available would be granted canonical status, that is, put in the Christian Bible. Since the Church was deciding which books were inspired by the Holy Spirit and which were not, it was imperative to believe that the Church was inspired by the Holy Spirit in this awesome undertaking. Once this was accomplished, so the argument goes, it was quite natural that the Church would feel competent to make authoritative interpretation of the Scriptures. The Church believed that the Holy Spirit continued to reveal the will of God through the Church. Since the Holy Spirit would not contradict himself, what was revealed to the Church would not contradict, but rather deepen and clarify, what was revealed in the Scriptures. The result was the anathematization of heresies and the formulation of creeds and doctrines—in short, the *development of doctrine*. Retrospectively, therefore, heresies are understood to be "illegitimate," extrainstitutional developments of doctrine.

But what was the Church? Who spoke for the Church? Generally the bishops spoke for the mind of the Church. Bishops were those churchmen who stood in communion with the great apostolic sees such as Alexandria, Rome, Antioch—that is, who stood in the *Apostolic Succession*. The authority of the Church and its tradition was guaranteed by the Holy Spirit through the Apostolic Succession of orthodox bishops.[2] It is the *Apostolic* Christians (mainly Roman Catholics, Eastern Orthodox, and Anglo-Catholics within the Anglican Communion) who accept the full authority of the seven Ecumenical Councils and practice (what they variously understand to be) the Apostolic Succession. Given our secular premise as to what constitutes normativeness, this Apostolic tradition is normative *simply because* it is *majoritarian*—and that in two ways: (1) chronologically, roughly seventy-five percent of Christian history has been virtually uniformly Apostolic; and (2) numerically, since the Reformation (when the Apostolic Succession was broken), Apostolic Christians have made up roughly seventy-five percent of all Christendom.

Our secular premise as to what constitutes normativeness happens to "validate" the entire Apostolic tradition. But for the purposes of this study, all that need be established is the normativeness of the Ecumenical Councils (actually, an acceptance of only the third council, the Council of Ephesus in 431, will suffice) as well as the tradition of the ("early") Church prior to the first council, the Council of Nicea in 325. This minimalist standard is sufficient for the purposes of this book because the heresies with which we are concerned were condemned either by the Council of Ephesus (Pelagianism) or by the early Church (Gnosticism and Montanism). (Whether or in what way one chooses to accept the tradition of the "undivided Church" from the time of the seventh Council in 787 to the official division of the Church in ca. 1054 is a moot issue. In what follows I shall speak of the Church with an uppercase "C" when speaking of the "undivided" Apostolic Church, but the church with a lowercase "c" when speaking of Christians after the great schism of ca. 1054.) The condemnation of Pelagianism, Gnosticism, and Montanism is certainly authoritative for Apostolic Christians (whatever their subsequent differences), that is, for the overwhelming majority of Christians. Since I have no desire to exclude Protestants from the picture, it should be mentioned that the Protestant witness to the authority of the Councils and the tradition of the early Church is not unanimous or unambiguous. Nevertheless, it can be said with assurance that the mainstream Reformers gathered around Luther and Calvin continued to regard Gnosticism, Montanism, and Pelagianism as heretical (but on purely scriptural grounds). Indeed, the same may be said of what today is loosely called "orthodox Protestantism."

Orthodoxy, as we shall be using the concept (namely, in regard to revelation, Original Sin, and the Kingdom of God), is, therefore, something common to Christians regardless of communion or denomination. But today there is a cleavage between orthodoxy and heterodoxy within the universal church. The cleavage does not usually separate one church from another, but cuts through virtually all churches. Today both orthodoxy and heresy are ecumenical.

But granted there is an ecumenical orthodoxy under attack by an ecumenical heresy, why is orthodoxy so important? Why have Christians historically seemed to be obsessed with orthodoxy (perhaps to the neglect of other Christian values)? Why does it matter so much that one have right belief? Heresy is a

threat to the Christian because Christianity is a salvation religion, salvation is largely a matter of faith, and the object of faith
is the Gospel. To distort the Gospel, which is the good news of
salvation, is to imperil salvation. Hence, heresy is a grave obstacle to salvation because it distorts the Gospel. That is why right
belief is so important for the Christian. Indeed, Harvey Cox,
himself something of an apologist for heresy, has complained
that "Christianity is perhaps the only religion with the idea of
belief; it is perhaps the only religion in the world where one
can equate adherents or followers with believers."[3]

Christians believe that the distinction between orthodoxy
and heresy corresponds to the distinction between truth and
error. Truth is, of course, a self-recommending value. What sane
person cherishes falsehood and delusion, and abhors truth? But
for the Christian, truth is of more than intrinsic value. First,
Christian truth is supposed to be truth about God. To advance
heresies is to lie about God, which is an offense against God.
Second, Christian truth has instrumental value in that what one
believes, in what one vests one's faith, is supposed to have an
overriding bearing on one's eternal salvation or eternal perdi-
tion.

The historic Apostolic Church has never said that what one
believes is of no matter because all will be saved in the end.
(The mainstream Reformers did not break with the Apostolic
Church on this point.) For example, the Athanasian Creed (ca.
450), one of the three great creeds of Christendom, was unequivocal on this point: "Whosoever will be saved: before all
things it is necessary that he hold the Catholic Faith: Which
Faith except every one do keep whole and undefiled: without
doubt he shall perish everlastingly."[4] In the early Church it was
Origen who championed the view that all people would be
saved in the end. However, the fifth Ecumenical Council, the
second Council of Constantinople in 553, condemned Origen

and universalism. However repugnant the Church's position may seem to the modern mind, it is important for those who minimize the importance of *orthodoxia* (or "right opinion") to realize that they are contradicting the testimony of historic Christianity. (It would be improper to conclude from the above that such qualities as love, good deeds, or a personal encounter with Jesus are unimportant for salvation to the orthodox Christian.)

Since this study has a linguistic orientation, it is appropriate to comment on the relation of the category of heresy to the nature of religious language. It is a philosophical commonplace that in speaking of supernatural mysteries one runs up against the boundaries of literal speech. For example, the cardinal Christian doctrines of Original Sin, the Incarnation, and the Trinity traffic in logical contradictions, more politely referred to as "paradoxes." It is characteristic of heretics to destroy those paradoxes. Take the Incarnation of Christ, for example. This doctrine presupposes an orthodox Christology. Christology is the branch of theology which deals with the nature of Christ. According to orthodox Christology, Jesus was both truly man and truly God at the same time. This is paradoxical, and it is not surprising that some (like the Docetists and Gnostics) could believe that Jesus was truly God but could not believe he was also truly man, while others (like the Arians and Pelagians) could believe he was truly man but found it impossible to believe he was also truly God. Now, just because the doctrine of the Incarnation (which presupposes an orthodox Christology) does not conform to ordinary standards of literal speech need not mean that the doctrine is only relatively true or that it might be superseded by a new formulation of the doctrine. To insist that orthodox formulations of doctrine should remain open to drastic alteration because of the nonliteral nature of religious language does not necessarily follow. To insist that Christian doctrines are relative and plastic because they are not literal is a philosophical absurdity. For the orthodox Christian, doctrines and discourse about divine mysteries are as true as "true" can be, given the nature of language. To yearn for some nonparadoxical expression of Christian truths, for some literal resolution of Christian paradoxes, is itself typical of the heretical impulse.

Wherever a religion affirms a distinction between natural and supernatural worlds, speech about the divinity will probably be laden with paradox. Where the reality of a supernatural world is denied, as is the case with many dialogical Christians, it would be much more difficult to excuse and dignify logical contradictions as "paradoxes."[5]

REVELATION: PROPHECY, PROVIDENCE, AND THE SPIRIT OF THE AGE

It is characteristic of dialogical Christians to announce new revelations from God, to announce that they are successors to the Old Testament prophets and enjoy special insight into God's providential will for the political arrangements of mankind. But unfortunately, given the historical standards of Christian orthodoxy, these self-styled modern prophets are probably not prophets at all, but rather false prophets.

This distinction between prophecy and false prophecy presupposes a conception of religious authority. For orthodox Christians, the authoritative source of revelation is the Bible as understood by the tradition of their church (this is further explained in my discussion of Montanism later in this section). Any alleged prophecies that occur in contemporary times must be tested for authenticity in terms of their conformity with authoritative revelation. Heterodox Christians often give recognition and/or priority to alternate sources of revelation. For example, if an alleged prophecy contradicts what is taught by the Bible and tradition, then the latter must be questioned.

There are growing numbers of "pentecostal" Christians who

make prophetic utterances on behalf of God. Usually these utterances are very personal and doctrinally conventional, hence of no threat to orthodoxy. The challenge to orthodoxy comes from those politicized Christians who, in seeming to mimic the prophetic mode, claim clairvoyance into the "politics of God," announce new and unprecedented revelations about the will of God, and try to press the church into conformity with their private political illuminations. These prophets probably must be considered heretics because they seem to prophesy, not on behalf of God, but on behalf of an alien god, in this case, the Zeitgeist.

The Zeitgeist is a notion often understood to be of Hegelian inspiration. It may be translated as the Spirit of the Age, the Spirit of the Times, or the Spirit of the present World. The Zeitgeist is an ontological imperative which possesses its own power and authority, and guides the direction of history. It is a reification; it is more than a collection of ideas, it is *the Idea*. It is more than the sum of its parts. It is more *Real* than real.

The Zeitgeist may be understood in a general or a specific sense. In a general sense it is the spirit of any given age. I choose to speak of it in a *specific* sense as the Spirit of the Modern Age (the time roughly since the Enlightenment). It is not my purpose to prove the existence of the Zeitgeist in the allegedly Hegelian sense. The Zeitgeist can be understood less metaphysically as simply the dominant intellectual ethos or spirit of a given time—which I take to be an unproblematic notion. However one chooses to understand the Zeitgeist, it is my thesis that the Spirit of the Modern Age is anti-Christian, and that dialogical Christians worship it by treating it as a new source of revelation, mistaking it for the Holy Spirit or Providence, and investing it with salvific significance. In its broadest sense our Zeitgeist is the messianic Idea of Progress, the yearning for the earthly New Jerusalem which—beginning with the

Enlightenment, as Louis I. Bredvold has indicated—has become "deeply ingrained . . . in the modern mind."[6] According to Helmut Gollwitzer, the Enlightenment was antagonistic to historical Christianity and constituted "the first high-water mark in the self-realization of the modern spirit." And, it is Marxism that "provides us with the most determined expression of the Enlightenment."[7]

It is instructive to contrast the secular messianism of modernity with the traditional Christian philosophy of history. According to Eric Voegelin, the Christian view distinguishes between

> a profane sphere of history in which empires rise and fall and a sacred history which culminates in the appearance of Christ and the establishment of the church . . . Only transcendental history, including the earthly pilgrimage of the church, has direction toward its eschatological fulfillment. Profane history, on the other hand, has no such direction; it is a waiting for the end . . . .[8]

Since modern culture could no longer swallow the notion of a transcendental history, it imputed the values, symbols, and prophecies of transcendental history to profane history. Providence was the architect of transcendental history and what the Enlightenment did was to *transform Providence into historical Progress,* the architect of which is mankind. With the progressive conquests of science and human reason, it seemed possible to translate heavenly promises into earthly realities. Hence, the urge to realize the Kingdom of God on earth came to be the hallmark of the modern sensibility.

Modernity endowed profane history with a transcendental purpose, direction, and destination of its own. Transcendence was collapsed and converted from a heavenly dimension (the "Above") into a dimension of this world, namely, the dimension of the future (the "Ahead"). The hope for perfection after death was transformed into the assertion of man's divinity in an earthly future. As Robert C. Tucker wrote:

> The movement of thought from Kant to Hegel revolved in a fundamental sense around the idea of man's self-realization as a god-like being or, alternately, as God. A radical departure from Western tradition was implicit in the tendency. The centuries-old ruling conception of an unbridgeable chasm of kind between the human and the divine gave way to the conception of a surmountable difference of degree. It is hardly surprising that out of such a revolution of religion there issued, among other things, a religion of revolution.[9]

This desire to reclaim the attributes of divinity for mankind—a desire best articulated by Ludwig Feuerbach—and to impute the characteristics of transcendental history to profane history is an act of hubris or arrogance from the viewpoint of traditional Christianity. It is the epitome of the sins of pride and idolatry, namely, the rejection of human finitude, and the divinization and worship of self. Once a supernatural God is denied and transcendence is made into a human dimension, the religious relationship to God is turned inside out and reappears as a "quasi-religious relationship to *the spirit of a secular age.*"[10]

The modern belief in Progress, whatever its original rationalistic underpinnings, does indeed manifest religious qualities. As a faith it seems remarkably impervious to repeated evidence of crisis and disaster. Because Progress is really the religion of modernity "it could not die with the guns of August [1914], nor with the Depression of the 30s, nor even with Auschwitz."[11]

Moreover, the Spirit of the Age is so pervasive and durable that, despite its anti-Christian thrust, it even works its way into the household of faith. One example of a Zeitgeist enthusiast in the church is Harvey Cox. Cox, who denies a supernatural God, contends that God reveals himself, not primarily in the Bible or church, but in the progressive historical and political events of the secular world. The Christian does not take God to the world, because God is already *visibly* present in the secular world. Cox identifies the Spirit of the world with God: "Only when we have learned the world's language can we speak of God. The world, its character, its hopes, its meaning, its destiny, becomes the *content* as well as the *context* of our speaking."[12] Clearly, the world must set the agenda for the church, for however the world understands itself *is* God. The world's secular, optimistic, and messianic self-understanding, its Spirit, is God. In seemingly Hegelian fashion, history is the autobiography of the Zeitgeist as it moves toward self-realization in the march of humanity toward the earthly New Jerusalem.

Since *Marxism* is the most dynamic expression of the secular messianism of our time—as Garaudy has said, "Marxism is not only a philosophy of our time. It is our time's *sense.*"[13]—dialogical Christians have been anxious to make peace with it. They have taken the dimension of *earthly futurity* as their theological point of departure and their *point of contact* with Marxism— and with the modern age in general. For example, Cox points out that millenarian preoccupation with the earthly future, while a marginal phenomenon limited to heretical sects during most of the history of Christendom, has now become "the mood of a whole culture."[14] Therefore, to relate Christianity to this mood, Cox seeks to recast the millenarian heretics as authentic Christians. Juergen Moltmann says that one of the common bases for dialogue with Marxism is the "eschatological interpretation of *modern times* as the dawning of the 'new age' and the 'new world.' "[15] Cox and Moltmann would agree with Garaudy when he says that the church must accept socialism and when he asks Christians "to be more fully Christian, i.e., to be able to give a Christian answer to the problems of our times and to give it *in the spirit of our times.*"[16] It is interesting that Garaudy has already described Marxism as the *sense* of our time; hence, a "Christian answer to the problems of our times" reduces itself to something not too different from a Marxist answer. That which is so widely hailed as a "dialogue" between Marxism and Christianity subtly becomes a monologue whereby Marxism assimilates Christianity into the dominant chorus of the times (suggesting once again that "synthetic dialogue" may be a contradiction in terms).

The difficulty with this reduction or secularization of Christianity, from E. L. Mascall's orthodox viewpoint, is that "it reduces the dialogue between Christianity and contemporary thought to a purely one-way process; there is no question of contemporary thought adapting itself to the Gospel, the Gospel must come into line entirely with contemporary thought."[17] However, Christianity's historical understanding of itself forbids a capitulation to the times. In the words of Karl Barth (generally regarded as the greatest Protestant theologian of the twentieth century), "the Church must not allow itself to be swept away by the movements of the age. . . ."[18] Even the usually broad-minded *Christian Century* found itself restating this historic position when it objected to the idea that the Lutheran bishops of Sweden should relax their condemnation of premarital sexual relations in order to get in step with Swedish society. The *Century* editorialized:

> If the church remains fixed to those eternal realities which are its authority, the church will often be out of step with the temporal realities. Paul's "Be not conformed to this world" requires that the church take its directions from something other than the customs of men. Neither in the realm of sexual relations nor elsewhere can "this present age" be trusted to fashion men's morals and the church's standards.[19]

Christians are frequently urged not to conform themselves to the "world" (or sometimes, more accurately, the "age"). Let us examine the normative Christian understanding of the world.

The Christian understanding must not be confused with the Gnostic understanding which holds the world to be totally evil. Rather, for the Christian the physical world (including the body), which is the world created by God, is good. Even after the Fall this essential goodness is not erased, although it is qualified. Evil enters the world through the Fall of Adam; however, this evil is of a *spiritual* nature. As St. Augustine said, "For gold is not evil, which God hath made; but the avaricious man is evil, who leaveth the Creator, and turneth to the creature."[20] Sin originates in the corruption of the heart; it is self-love, pride, greed, lust, and wanting to be godlike (as when the Serpent said to Eve in the Garden, "ye shall be as gods"). It is not the substance of the flesh which is evil, but the "works of the flesh"—which originate with the heart or will. Contrary to the Greek and Gnostic views, the good soul does not sin because of a bad body, rather the good body sins because of a wicked heart.[21]

When the New Testament refers positively to the world, the word *kosmos* is most frequently used, suggesting the physical world. When it refers to the world negatively, the word *aiōn* is used, suggesting "world spirit" or "fallen age" (or *kosmos* is qualified with the word "fallen").[22] This distinction between a good *kosmos* and a corrupted *aiōn* again points to the spiritual nature of sin, to the goodness of the created order but the wickedness of the spirit of the age—which is the wicked heart writ large. This is why orthodox Christians may not take their standards from the Zeitgeist, from the Spirit of the Age—this age or any other. This is also why they would regard the deification of the Spirit of the Modern Age as idolatrous, for that Spirit is a creation of the creature, hence a "graven image."

As one of Pope Paul's favorite theologians, Jacques Maritain, has pointed out, it is a deviant understanding of "the world" which is at the root of much of dialogical Christianity. Maritain excoriated the tendency to betray the Gospel by "kneeling before the world." By that he meant roughly, the "chronolatrous" worship of the Zeitgeist. "What do we find at the origin of this kneeling?" he asked. In a passage that merits lengthy quotation, he answered:

> An insane mistake—the confusion between two completely different senses in which the same word "world" is being understood.
>
> There is . . . an "ontosophic truth" about the world considered in its natural structures or in what properly constitutes it; in this sense we must say that the world is fundamentally *good.* [This corresponds to the good *kosmos.*]
>
> And there is a "religious" or "mystical" truth about the world considered in its ambiguous relationship to the kingdom of God and the Incarnation. Then we must say that the world, insofar as it accepts to be assumed into the kingdom, is *saved;* while insofar as it refuses the kingdom, and encloses itself in the lust of the flesh, the lust of the eyes, and the pride of the spirit, it is the *adversary* of Christ and his disciples, and *hates* them. [This corresponds to the corrupted *aiōn.*]
>
> Well, when people muddle these two understandings of the word "world," by imagining that the first truth concerning the world destroys the second . . . then it is the world itself which is the kingdom of God, in a state of becoming (and, at the final end, in glory). And it hasn't the slightest need to be saved from above, nor to be assumed and finally transfigured in Another world, a divine world. . . . It is from within . . . that the world will be saved, or rather that it saves itself and exalts itself. Down on your knees, then, with Hegel and his followers, before this illusory world; to it our faith, our hope, our love![23]

Hence, the Christian has no reason to flee from the physical world, but has every reason to run from the worldly spirit—whether lodged in his heart or embodied in the Zeitgeist.

One of the major themes of dialogical Christianity—and one of Cox's persistent claims—is that God is a "politician-God" who works through the progressive political events of the day.

At issue here, of course, is whether this God is the providential God of Christianity or the Zeitgeist. According to Cox, politics must replace metaphysics as the language about God. The church is not the locus of divine action, rather it is the agency which, through reflection and worldly involvement, "finds out what this politician-God is up to and moves in to work along with him."[24] Cox has changed his mind about various matters, but he has never had difficulty in spotting the hand of God in sociopolitical events. He has said that evidence of the breaking in of God's Kingdom could be found in the Freedom Schools set up in the heyday of the civil rights movement, in Saul Alinsky's Woodlawn experiment, and in the integration of professional baseball.[25] More recently, he has pointed to the Kingdom in the liberation of the natural environment from man's greed and the liberation of children, as well as the modified monogamy of Margaret Mead's "cluster family" idea and the transcendence of the nation-state system.[26]

Sometimes it is not the Kingdom of God, but the Holy Spirit's activity, which is perceived, as when former Catholic priest Philip Berrigan said in 1968: "You see the Spirit is not chained! My friend George McGovern has declared himself for the Presidency. I only hope that this move will help McCarthy take the scene."[27] McCarthy did not take the scene; however, Berrigan continued in the prophetic mode: "Yes, man is really coming to a full self-consciousness. . . . the Holy Spirit is working through today's communication media and technology, making people aware of their plight, and revolting against it."[28] Garry Wills elegantly diagnosed this mentality when he said that "some proponents of modernity . . . seem convinced that the Spirit of the Age and the Holy Spirit have somehow intermingled flames. . . ."[29]

In general, dialogical Christians tend to see the hand of God in the rise of Communism (frequently deemed a judgment of

God upon the sins of the capitalist West), the violent revolutions of oppressed Third World peoples, the peace movement, the student movement, the women's movement, and the black movement.[30] In fact, wherever the Zeitgeist is working itself out, there is God. Wherever people, responding to the imperatives of the age, are involved in allegedly noble and uplifting pursuits, God is with them almost by definition. The guiding principle of this way of thinking was expressed half a century ago by the leading light in the American Social Gospel movement, Walter Rauschenbusch, when he said, "The gospel, to have full power over an age, must be the highest expression of the moral and religious truths held by that age." He urged the churches to support "the high patriotic and social ambitions" of the age.[31] Curiously, it was this kind of logic that allowed Lord Rosebery to sing the praises of the British Empire in such effusive terms as these:

> How marvelous it all is! Built not by saints and angels, but the work of men's hands; cemented with men's honest blood and with a world of tears, welded by the best brains of the centuries past; not without the taint and reproach incidental to all human work, but constructed on the whole with pure and splendid purpose. *Human and yet not wholly human,* for the most heedless and the most cynical must see *the finger of the Divine.*[32]

It was also this kind of logic which led the *Deutsche Christen,* the pro-Hitler "German-Christians," to support the ambitions of National Socialism, to the point of regarding it as a new revelation from God. Today it is an uncontested truth that the German-Christian phenomenon was treacherous and lamentable. Why? Because it aided Hitler, yes, but also because it perverted and polluted the Gospel by injecting an alien element, namely, *Germanism.* What the German-Christians had asserted was that Hitler's assumption of power was an act of divine redemption and a new source of divine revelation. In the words of Barth, "beside the Holy Scriptures as the unique source of revelation, the German-Christians affirm the German nationhood, its history and its contemporary political situation as a *second source of revelation,* and thereby betray themselves to be believers in 'another God.'"[33]

Barth was the leader of the neo-orthodox movement in Continental Protestant theology. He stood for the sovereignty of a transcendent God and the authority of the Scriptures. He did battle with the religious liberals who sought to immanentize God, cast doubt on the reliability of the Scriptures, and enlist religion in the service of what were thought to be man's noble endeavors. According to H. Richard Niebuhr, religious liberals sought to prove religion's usefulness to man "in promoting the dominant purposes of the age or group in which they lived, the purposes of nationalism where nationalism was in power, of capitalism where capitalism reigned, of radicalism where radicalism took the initiative."[34] And, it must be added, National Socialism where National Socialism prevailed. It should be remembered that Nazism appeared for a long time to many Germans (and non-Germans) as a noble cause, as the wave of the future, even perhaps as the embodiment of the Spirit of the Age.

Liberal religion is frequently a defensive attempt to seek an accommodation with the outlook of the secular world. Such a secular-minded and man-centered theology refuses to set itself up against the ascendent presuppostions of the day. In the case before us, it led to the Nazifying of the German churches of the Reformation. Franklin H. Littell described the problem well:

> The Liberal Theology had done much to disintegrate the theological integrity of the Protestant Churches. Activity in the field of social reform was taking the place of witness to the Gospel of Redemption. And there were those who were willing to fill the void created by their own disbelief by political enthusiasms—en-

thusiasm for Socialism, or, in the situation of 1933, for National Socialism. It was from these people that the so-called "German Christians" emerged.[35]

What Barth had done was to direct his fire against "the dominant liberalism, which saw the divine in immanent continuity with the 'best' and the 'highest' in man's spirit and culture, so that talking about God did indeed become, as Barth was later to comment so caustically, 'talking about man in a loud voice.'"[36]

More recently, the second-source-of-revelation heresy has been a temptation to Christians sympathetic to Marxism-Leninism. One of the clearest cases is represented by Albert Berecsky, the Reformed bishop of Hungary. Berecsky not only perceived the hand of God in secular history, but subordinated the Christian drama of salvation to Communism by treating Communism as an epiphany of God and elevating it into a vehicle of salvation.[37]

Barth, who strongly defended Berecsky's progressive political views, rose to express his deep suspicion of Berecsky's theological position, which he associated with false prophecy and a second revelation. Barth warned: "you are on the way to making your affirmation of communism a part of the Christian message, an article of faith which . . . threatens to overshadow all other articles of faith, and on the basis of which you would now interpret the whole creed and the whole Bible. In other words, you are falling into that ideological-Christian way of thinking which once, under different auspices, was adopted by the 'German Christians.'"[38]

The German-Christians saw the "finger of the Divine" in the Nazi revolution, Lord Rosebery saw it in the British Empire, and Berecsky saw it in the rise of Communism. Cox, carrying on this tradition, sees it in the integration of professional baseball and children's liberation, et al. Since the causes endorsed are so various and contradictory it is unlikely that all of them represent

God's will. Then what "objective" *Christian* criterion is there by which to judge when and where God is, and is not, acting in profane history? Given the standards of orthodoxy, it would seem that there is no criterion whatsoever by which judgments of this kind could be rendered. One is forced to conclude that judgments of this nature—whether of the "right," "center" or "left"—are probably products of exacerbated political passions and/or naive prejudices.

From the viewpoint of orthodoxy, the problem here is that there is a mistaken view whereby Providence is regarded as manifest rather than mysterious. When Providence is equated with one's own understanding of man's noblest designs and achievements, then the temptation is overwhelming to see God supporting one's own favorite political projects. Notions of a manifest Providence are probably always self-serving. The result is an idolatrous second source of revelation which rivals or supersedes the authoritative source of revelation—Bible and church. Adherents of a manifest Providence are oblivious to the mysterious ways of God, as expressed in the words of the prophet: "For my thoughts are not your thoughts, and your ways are not my ways. This is the very word of the LORD" (Isaiah 55:8 NEB), and by St. Paul: "O depth of wealth, wisdom, and knowledge of God! How unsearchable his judgements, how untraceable his ways! Who knows the mind of the Lord? Who has been his counsellor?" (Romans 11:33–34 NEB). Indeed, the philosopher of history Karl Loewith has observed that "the Hebrew-Christian tradition . . . obstructs the attempt to 'work out' the working of God."[39]

The second-source-of-revelation heresy found its classic expression and authoritative repudiation in Montanism. Of course, the establishment of a second source of revelation is typical of major heresies. However, Montanism is the archetype because it was condemned not so much because of *what* it claimed on the basis of its new source of revelation as for the reason *that* it claimed for itself a new source of revelation.

Montanism was not condemned because it was prophetic, but because of the revelational status it claimed for its prophecies. In the early Church, Christian prophets (charismatics who uttered direct communications from God somewhat in the fashion of the Old Testament prophets) were recognized as a legitimate tradition. Montanus took this legitimate "pentecostal" tradition and corrupted it. He indicated that he regarded himself as the Paraclete, the Holy Spirit incarnate, hence as a "new revelation [which] went beyond all the preceding ones, even those of Christ and the apostles."[40] Montanus placed the Holy Spirit (actually himself) above Scriptures and Church as the authoritative source of revelation. This was what might be called a unitarianism of the Third Person.

But Montanus was initiating a new era as well as a new revelation. He identified the coming of the Holy Spirit, not with Pentecost as the orthodox did, but with himself. The Montanists "went so far as to announce that there were three separate dispensations, corresponding with the three Persons of the Trinity."[41] In this, they anticipated Joachim di Fiore (to be discussed below). Montanists believed God had failed to redeem the world through the revelation of the Father or of the Son, and hence God sent a new revelation, namely, the Holy Spirit through the medium of Montanus himself.

The Church did not regard Montanus as an innocent visionary, but rather as a demonic threat. Montanism, which began as an admirable attempt to purify the Church, ended as an attack on the basic Christian understanding of the nature of revelation. As a result, Montanus was excommunicated from the Church in 177. Both Apostolic and mainline Protestant Christianity have endorsed this condemnation.

Montanism is a prescription for doctrinal anarchy. As a revelational method it means that anyone claiming inspiration from the Holy Spirit can claim for himself a new revelation. The notion of divine revelation becomes a hopeless web of confusion. The need for a standard of authority regarding alleged inspiration from the Holy Spirit was expressed in the New Testament: "But do not trust any and every spirit, my friends; test the spirits, to see whether they are from God, for among those who have gone out into the world there are many prophets falsely inspired" (1 John 4:1 NEB). The Church tackled this problem early. It decided that a false prophet is one whose illuminations either contradict or are not warranted by the Scriptures as interpreted by the Apostolic Church, and who proceeds to regard his illuminations as normative for the whole Church. The critical point is that the Church decided to subordinate prophecy to its own Apostolic authority: "The Apostles were the successors of the prophets [of the Old Testament]; they were prophets invested with supreme authority. . . . The apostolate was succeeded, not by another prophetism but by the Church: the reign of continuity, succession, and the normative institution to which the prophets are subject. . . . In the time of the Church the 'prophetic office' never ceased. But the prophets rose up and acted within the Church."[42] The Reformers, of course, rejected the Apostolic tradition and Apostolic Succession; however, their followers came to act on an analogous principle, namely, that whatever contradicts or is not warranted by the Scriptures as interpreted by the Lutheran and/or Calvinist traditions (which appropriated much of the base of the Apostolic tradition) is falsely inspired. Hence, the differences between Apostolic and Protestant Christians are minor compared with what separates both of them from the proponents of alien sources of revelation.

Alien sources of revelation and notions of manifest Providence are closely tied in with the concept of prophecy. It is frequently through the prophet that God reveals his will. That is, it is the prophet who enjoys the special gift of discerning God's ways and pronouncing his judgment. Modeling themselves on the Old Testament prophets, dialogical Christians often announce God's purposes in history and bring his judgment upon the excesses of capitalism, the oppressors of Third World peoples, warmongers, university bureaucrats, male chauvinists, polluters, and white racists. The mark of a true prophet, Paul Ramsey said sarcastically, is to prophesy against the government and/or the right wing.[43]

This kind of prophecy can come fast and furious. It has sometimes been called "cheap" prophecy because it is often made so easily (although in some cases with great personal risk). This urge for instant prophecy is frequently indulged in when councils of churches meet and denominations hold their conventions. Delegates are implored to involve themselves in the issues of the day in a truly prophetic manner. Resolutions are passed and submitted to the press. Perhaps the reason why this kind of prophecy comes so effortlessly is that the point of reference is not some inscrutable God of history, but the Spirit of the Age—the content of which is open to anyone who cares to inquire.

Ironically, this desire to emulate the Hebrew prophets usually misses the authentic spirit of prophecy: "A prophet is a man through whom God speaks. This is one of the most awesome fates that could befall a human being, and it is usually accompanied by great suffering. Not surprisingly, most of the prophets appearing in the Bible strenuously resisted this vocation. They finally accepted it because they could no longer resist God. This is not only awesome. It is humanly terrible." These are the words of Peter Berger, disclaiming the honorific title of "angry young prophet" which had been affixed to him and his work. For him to regard his activity as prophetic, he said, would be "blasphemous."[44]

One reason why traditional Christians are so anxious to disavow, rather than assume, the prophetic mantle, is that they know that true prophecy is a radically uncommon event and that Providence is essentially mysterious. Said Abraham J. Heschel of Hebrew prophecy: "Prophecy is a moment of unshrouding, an opening of the eyes, a lifting of the curtain. Such moments are rare in history."[45] The fact that modern prophecy is such a widespread activity is circumstantial evidence that it is not lodged on behalf of God. (To be sure, modern prophets attack unjust institutions and habits, and champion the poor. But this is only a derivative aspect of the authentic prophetic function. To champion the poor does not make one ipso facto a prophet. For example, the prophet Jeremiah did not champion the poor—or the rich—when he told his people to surrender to the Babylonians. Furthermore, simply to be for "the good" does not make one ipso facto a prophet either. Said Reinhold Niebuhr: "The prophet throws all symbols of human *goodness* out of the Temple."[46])

In short, the mark of a true prophet is to speak the authoritative and binding word of God, even to the point of pain and suffering. This is an imposing, perhaps dreadful, event. According to Gerhard von Rad:

> there is universal agreement, that visions and auditions came to the prophets from outside themselves, and that they came suddenly and completely without premeditation. . . . There is no doubt that, at the moment when the prophets received a revelation, they believed that they heard themselves addressed in words . . . .very frequently at least, such reception of revelation was something which caused the prophet a severe bodily shock. . . . Ezekiel relates how he sat on the ground awe-struck and unable to speak a word for seven days after his call (Ezek. 3:15).[47]

The prophet does not speak for himself, he does not announce what *he* thinks is just or good; rather, he speaks for God. Any other seemingly prophetic trait (other than, in the Christian context, conformity with the original source of revelation) is incidental.

Modern self-styled prophets are primarily intellectuals (usually seminary or religion professors, ecclesiastical officials, and religious journalists) who, unlike ordinary parish clergy, are free from pressures exerted by rank and file church members. Their concerns are primarily those of the secular progressive intellectuals. According to Seymour Martin Lipset and Richard B. Dobson, "the leaders of the churches . . . conceive of themselves as 'intellectuals' and include the secular intellectuals in their reference group. The leaders of the churches appear to seek the approbation of the intellectual community. . . . theology has become a subbranch of the broader intellectual life."[48] Inasmuch as it is the secular progressive intellectuals who nourish, promote, and define the Zeitgeist, it is not surprising to see our modern prophets act as agents of the Zeitgeist.

Lest this sound like a caricature, allow me to cite the words of Daniel Callahan, one of the most prestigious progressive Catholic intellectuals in America. What he says deserves lengthy quotation:

> there is a very real danger in the way left-wing Catholicism has become so respectable among secular intellectuals. I am writing this at a very nice desk, in a very nice house, and most of the money for these amenities has come from the unsought but profitable business of being known as a left-wing OK Catholic, one who can be counted on to knock the same things in the Church that most enlightened secular minds have always knocked. . . . The game of being more-radical-than-thou is a big one in left-wing Catholicism. The coincidence between this radicalism and upper-level main-line secular American intellectual values is worthy of continual suspicion. On the whole, I don't think I will be happy with left-wing Catholicism until it has learned how to be prophetic to the upper-strata of American secular liberalism; at present, we are just trailing along behind, happy to provide it our

theological blessing. It is not hard at all to be prophetic in the face of conservative Christianity; or in the face of a status quo racist, war-mongering society; or in the face of bureaucratic bishops. But it is extraordinarily hard to be prophetic to hippies, New Leftists, and those who are already with-it to an extraordinary degree.[49]

In sum, the orthodox Christian is one who is extremely skeptical of those *Zeitgeist mitlaeufer,* those "OK Christians," those "prophets," who are able to spot the "finger of the Divine" in political events, who sacralize human Progress, immanentize the New Jerusalem, and speak a word, not from God, but from the Spirit of the Times.

ORIGINAL SIN AND PROMETHEUS

According to the doctrine of Original Sin, man is partly corrupt and limited in what he can achieve. Man inevitably sins and is incapable of saving himself. One of the cardinal sins is pride, which was the "original" sin of Adam and Eve. For man to deny and defy his finitude, and to try to be what he cannot be (namely, God) is to be guilty of the Promethean sin of pride. To repudiate his dependence on God and build Towers of Babel is to commit the ultimate sin of rejecting God, that is, atheism.

It is this pessimistic doctrine against which modernity has rebelled. According to Reinhold Niebuhr: "Modern man does not regard life as tragic. He thinks that history is the record of the progressive triumph of good over evil. He does not recognize the simple but profound truth that man's life remains self-contradictory in its sin, no matter how high human culture rises. . . ."[50] Those who acknowledge Original Sin would argue that because modern culture is pridefully utopian in outlook it fails to see that self-interest corrupts even the most rational, moral, idealistic, and universalistic of natural man's enterprises. Modernity, which optimistically asserts its self-sufficiency, involves itself in the sin of pride. Not surprisingly, Garaudy has asked the church to rethink the notion of Original Sin as pride so that the church might accept, in his words, "the spirit of our age."[51]

The doctrine of Original Sin puts Christianity in clear opposition to Marxism, the most determined advocate of the values of modernity. According to the American Communist theoretician Herbert Aptheker, some of the most basic distinctions between Marxism and Christianity appear over the question of human nature. The Marxist estimate of man is "as like to a god," whereas the dominant note of Christianity is the contrary: "Man is puerile, unknowing, with pride his greatest failing and . . . the Fall induces innate and ineradicable proclivity to sin. . . ."[52] What separates Marxists from Christians here also separates normative Christians from dialogical Christians—who tend to endorse the Marxist position. For example, Cox said: "man's most debilitating proclivity is *not* his pride. It is *not* his attempt to be more than man. Rather it is his sloth, his unwillingness to be everything man was intended to be."[53] Likewise, Moltmann has said: "Temptation then consists not so much in the titanic desire to be as God, but in weakness, timidity, weariness. . . ."[54] Significantly, Garaudy observes that dialogical Christians are coming to see man as Marxists see him, that is, as "a budding god."[55]

In the early Church, it was primarily the Pelagians who rejected the doctrine of Original Sin. Pelagianism was anathematized as heresy by the Church at the third Ecumenical Council, the Council of Ephesus in 431.

Like the doctrines of the Incarnation and the Trinity, the doctrine of Original Sin is paradoxical. It holds that man inevitably sins, yet man is responsible for his sins. Man is not free and yet he is treated as if he were. The doctrine seeks to explain both why there is evil (because man *chooses* to sin) and why man must always look to God for salvation (because man *must* sin). It is characteristic of heretics to be intolerant of paradoxical doctrines. They seek to rationalize that which is not rational. For example, the Gnostics could believe that man is inevitably trapped in evil; however, they could not therefore affix any blame to man. They rejected Original Sin because they did not believe man in his heart was responsible for evil; they did not believe he was a sinner. The Pelagians could believe that man was responsible for his sins; however, they could not believe therefore that sin is involuntary.

Pelagians tended to adhere to a heretical Arian (or Adoptionist) Christology. That is, they did not believe that Jesus was God incarnate; rather, they believed that Jesus was an exceptionally good man, so good that God "adopted" him as his Son. The Pelagian God, like the Gnostic God, was infinitely remote from man, so much so that it was inconceivable that God could become man. Like the Gnostics (who believed Jesus was God but not really a man), the Pelagians believed man could become godlike. They believed that every man is as free as Adam was in deciding whether to sin or not. They believed that there were sinless men before Christ and that there could be sinless men after Christ, perhaps even worthy of adoption by God. Clearly, Christ loses his uniqueness and his finality.

Pelagius so strongly asserted man's freedom of the will that it was unnecessary to rely on the grace of God to achieve sinless perfection. Hence, salvation was not redemption from sin as orthodox Christians understand it. (Thus, the centrality of Christ's Atonement disappears.) Instead, the Pelagians, like the Gnostics, ultimately conceived of salvation as self-deification rather than as forgiveness. When this notion of self-salvation is applied collectively, it becomes a question of political self-salvation, which immediately suggests the imperative to construct the New Jerusalem, the Kingdom of God, on earth.

ESCHATOLOGY, THE NEW JERUSALEM, AND THE KINGDOM OF GOD

The belief that the building of the Kingdom of God can be initiated by human action is a modern heresy, and therefore it is not possible to point to its explicit condemnation by the early Church or by one of the Ecumenical Councils. Nevertheless, it should be noted that this belief has never had a place in orthodox theology, and that the condemnations of Pelagianism (see above) and Gnosticism (see below) at least implicitly discredit the notion that the building of the Kingdom can be initiated by mankind. In confirming the heterodox status of this belief I shall rely substantially on the views of prominent Christians who are commonly thought to hold an orthodox eschatology (that is, doctrine of the Last Things).

The Kingdom of God is a difficult doctrine and there is considerable liberty of opinion among the orthodox concerning it. According to the *premillennial* view, the apocalyptic Second Coming of Christ will immediately *precede* the millennial or thousand-year reign of Christ and his Saints on earth, after which the final Day of Judgment will occur. When the expectation of the millennium is imminent, premillennialism becomes chiliastic. Premillennialism is a minoritarian point of view despite its wide acceptance in the early Church. There does not seem to be anything heretical about it, although it has served as a jumping-off point for numerous heretics. Such an eschatology brings this world and the world to come (as a once-and-for-all event) into close proximity. This proximity has invited heretics—particularly during times of chiliastic excitement—to try to build bridges between their earthly cities and the New Jerusalem, to try to usher in the latter by revolutionizing the former. Premillennialism becomes heterodox when it is thought that man can play a decisive role in constructing the Kingdom—or trigger it (that is, force God's hand). Eschatology then slides into social revolution (as in the case of Thomas Muentzer), as the role of God is either denied or preempted. It is this heretical premillennialism—often chiliastic in form—which seems to inspire the eschatological politics of Cox and Moltmann.

The political climate of the 1960s and early 1970s was unusually apocalyptic and millennial in temper. The eschatologies of

Cox and Moltmann reflected that temper. However, on occa-
sion, Cox and Moltmann strike a more relaxed, more gradualist,
posture. When they do, their eschatologies may be characterized as *postmillennial* instead of premillennial. The orthodox
version of postmillennialism holds that the Second Coming of
Christ will occur *after* the millennium. During the millennium,
Satan will be bound, the Christian church will grow in strength
and influence, and human life will generally improve due to an
outpouring of God's grace. Postmillennial writers often argue
that the millennium is occurring *now*. In this sense, postmillennial eschatology goes beyond premillennialism because it usually holds not that this world and the next are in close proximity,
but that they have already intermingled—although the world to
come has not yet entirely defeated this present world. When
one adds the notion that God acts, not through the church, but
through the world and its history—as Cox and Moltmann clearly
do—then postmillenialism invites a de facto Pelagianism because, although God is supposedly responsible for human progress, it is impossible to know with any degree of certainty what
God is doing (see my discussion of Providence above). Hence,
it is easily assumed that whatever is approved by humans is
necessarily of God. And yet, it is quite apparent that the progress that is achieved is achieved by human effort. Man and his
desires and standards become the focus of attention. The idea
that God is behind it all easily slips into obscurity.

Today orthodox postmillennialism is virtually moribund (indeed, it never did have many adherents). The twentieth century
has been marked by calamity and crisis; it has not seen the
church march from triumph to triumph. On empirical grounds
alone, it is most difficult to make the case for the postmillennial
position. Moreover, among biblical scholars (whether "orthodox" or not), there is a clear consensus that postmillennialism
(even an orthodox version) was not the eschatology of Jesus—
not to speak of the early Church. Finally, postmillennialism suffers from its incompatibility with what is generally recognized

to be the Christian view of history (see my discussion of the Zeitgeist above).

Although Cox and Moltmann do sound postmillennial themes at times, their eschatological views are more premillennial than postmillennial. They do not tend to see this world and the world to come as intermingled in actuality; rather they see them in proximity. The Kingdom does not grow gradually through history; rather it breaks in radically from the future. Although they point to certain "signs" of the in-breaking Kingdom, they experience the Kingdom more as imminent expectation than as slow accomplishment. Nevertheless, their eschatological views are heterodox because ultimately they focus on what man can do, not what God will do. (Both postmillennialism and premillennialism become heterodox when the agency of transformation is naturalistic, that is, the force of history and/or man himself rather than God.) When Cox and Moltmann do talk of what "God" will do or is doing, they go far beyond what the traditional sources of revelation will allow. Hence, as I have argued above, their transcendental point of reference is not God, but the Zeitgeist.

The majoritarian view on eschatology in both Apostolic and Protestant Christianity has been the *amillennialism* inaugurated by St. Augustine. According to this view, there is strictly speaking no earthly millennium. The millennial Kingdom is understood figuratively and is largely regarded as already embodied on earth in the church or fellowship of believers (but *not* in the world at large). Hence, the New Jerusalem is not a millennial Kingdom on earth ruled by Christ and his Saints, but simply heaven (with all its otherworldly connotations). The Second Coming of Christ which will mark the end of the world is still expected someday, but it is not usually a focus of attention (as is the case with chiliastic premillennialism).

It becomes inordinately difficult to talk about man's building of the Kingdom with these amillennial presuppositions because heaven signifies a place where one hopes to go after one dies, not a new condition of life on earth. Hence, there does not seem to be a naturalistic or heretical version of this eschatology. Historically, the practical results of this view have been twofold: (1) the present world is not expected to pass away imminently, hence Christians become more reconciled to the world as it is, and (2) a sharp distinction arises between this world and the next so that, paradoxically, Christians also become more otherworldly. In sum, the world is accepted for what it is (not for what it might become), whereas ultimate hope is vouchsafed elsewhere.

To replace the distinction between sacred and profane history, the Kingdom of God and the Kingdom of man—above all, between the action of God and the action of man—with a fluid continuity and amalgamation is characteristic of heretical eschatologies. But, according to Martin D'Arcy, even in the early Church where a premillennial eschatology prevailed, "there is little or no trace of the view that the Christian Kingdom of God and the earthly Kingdom are intended to be one. . . . Without a break the doctrine of the two cities or Kingdoms developed. . . . Christianity, as we know, suffered divisions, but not on this point."[56]

The *indispensable* element in the orthodox view of the Kingdom (whether or not it involves an earthly millennium) is that it is built when God chooses, not when man chooses, and by God, not by man (even though God may use human agents). In Barth's words, "the *heavenly* State is and remains exclusively the *heavenly* State, established not by man but by God, which, as such, is not capable of realization in this age. . . ."[57] According to Pope Paul, the "proper growth [of the kingdom of God] cannot be confounded with the progress of civilization, of science or of human technology. . . ."[58] This is so because, according to official Roman theology, the eschatological Kingdom "will be the effect solely of divine intervention."[59]

In what follows I elaborate somewhat on this normative Christian view of the Kingdom. One of the reasons why the Jews rejected Christ was because they had a preconception of the Messiah that was not fulfilled by Jesus. The Jews expected a political and military Messiah who would conquer Israel's enemies and set up a theocratic political order. According to Oscar Cullmann, however, "the Jewish theocratic ideal is expressly rejected by Christianity as satanic—we need only recall the temptation stories in the Gospel. Satan offers to Christ the kingdoms of the world . . . . The Gospel knows nothing of that confusion of the Kingdom of God with the State which is characteristic of the theocratic ideal of Judaism."[60] The theocratic ideal found its sharpest expression in the Zealot movement. It is "quite possible," said Cullmann, that Judas Iscariot was a Zealot.

> If Judas was a member of the Zealot party, then we can understand his betrayal [of Jesus] much more simply. For he would then have had a messianic ideal quite different from Jesus' [which was otherworldly]; and his entry into the circle of disciples would have rested on a misapprehension of the goal Jesus was pursuing. Like others of the disciples, he would have pictured Jesus' role . . . as that of a messiah-king . . . a king who would bring the Roman rule to an end and thus establish the kingdom of God on earth."[61]

Jesus regarded the Zealot movement as a temptation and of the Devil, and he perceived the political conception of the Messiah as his special temptation. For Jesus, "the Kingdom of God is not brought in by human power, nor is it set up as a political kingdom."[62] His Kingdom "comes from God . . . ."[63]

"There is a growing consensus in New Testament scholarship," wrote George Eldon Ladd, "that the Kingdom of God is in some sense both present and future."[64] The Kingdom comes in two stages, each stage being inaugurated by God's supernatural intervention in history. The Kingdom first entered history in the Incarnation of Jesus Christ, to be continued through the community of believers and the church. In this sense the Kingdom is present. However, in this form the Kingdom is mysterious, since it does not alter the fallen nature of the world. The old age, the old structure of society, persists. Wrote Ladd: "Here is the mysterious fact about the Kingdom. Its blessings have entered the old age, introducing a new order of life which nevertheless does not bring the old order to its end for all men. The new order is not just the age to come, the Eschaton, but is a new order hidden in the old age. However, the new order, hidden as it was, brought salvation to its recipients but judgment to those who rejected it (Matt. 11: 20–24)"[65] The second and final stage of the Kingdom comes at the end of the world and is inaugurated by Christ's Second Coming. God intervenes to terminate history, destroy or transform the old order, and create a new heaven and a new earth. This is the eschatological consummation of all things. The Kingdom sheds its mysterious guise and appears in its fullness. In this sense the Kingdom is still in the future.

It is imperative to emphasize once again that when the Kingdom comes in its fullness, it comes by an act of God, not man. Ladd said: "It is pure miracle and entirely in God's hands. Man cannot compel or prevent its coming." "It is significant," he added, "that Jesus said nothing about building the Kingdom or of his disciples bringing in the Kingdom. . . . Evil is so radical that it can be overcome only by the mighty intervention of God."[66]

It should be apparent that the orthodox understanding of the Kingdom of God—as sketched above with the help of Ladd, Cullmann, and others—and the orthodox understanding of

Original Sin are related. If the Pelagian position is correct and Original Sin is unreal, then it might be possible for man to construct his Kingdom on earth. However, if Original Sin is real, then man must wait upon God's grace, which in its eschatological dimension means waiting upon his world-transforming action. Hence, for the orthodox Christian, any Promethean political ambition must be eschewed. Politics is a part of profane history. In the view of eternity, profane history ultimately has no future of and unto itself; it can never project itself into sacred history (although some orthodox Christians believe that certain aspects of profane history may, in the Eschaton, be transformed and perfected by God's grace and finally assimilated into the Kingdom of God). What remains clear is that man can only wait for the termination of profane history—which will come in God's good time and by means of his sovereign action.

NOTES

1. Vincenz von Lerinum, *Commonitorium* (Freiburg i. B. und Leipzig: Mohr, 1895), II: 3: 20–22 (the translation from the Latin is mine). For a standard English version, see Vincent of Lerins, "The Commonitories," *The Fathers of the Church* (New York: Fathers of the Church, Inc., 1949), 7: p. 270.

2. See Jaroslav Pelikan, *The Christian Tradition: A History of the Development of Doctrine, Vol. 1: The Emergence of the Catholic Tradition (100–600)* (Chicago: University of Chicago Press, 1971), pp. 68–71. Pelikan is a Lutheran. For a classically Catholic statement on tradition and the development of doctrine, see John Henry Cardinal Newman, *An Essay on the Development of Christian Doctrine* (Westminster, Md.: Christian Classics, 1968).

3. Harvey Cox, in *The Culture of Unbelief*, Rocco Caporale and Antonio Grumelli, eds. (Berkeley: University of California Press, 1971), p. 91.

4. See Philip Schaff, ed., *The Creeds of Christendom* (New York: Harper & Brothers, 1877), II: pp. 66ff.

5. For elaboration, see Dale Vree, "Reflections on Wittgenstein, Reli-

gion, and Politics," *Christian Scholar's Review, III*, No. 2 (1973), pp. 113–133.

6. Louis I. Bredvold, *The Brave New World of the Enlightenment* (Ann Arbor: University of Michigan Press, 1961), p. 102. The origins of our Zeitgeist can be traced back to the heterodox medieval chiliasts. See Karl Mannheim, *Ideology and Utopia* (New York: Harvest, 1936), pp. 211ff.

7. Helmut Gollwitzer, *The Christian Faith and the Marxist Criticism of Religion* (New York: Scribner's, 1970), pp. 4, 3. It should be noted that Gollwitzer has been a leading Christian advocate of Marxist-Christian dialogue in Europe. Also see John Courtney Murray, "The Freedom of Man in the Freedom of the Church," *Modern Catholic Thinkers*, A. Robert Caponigri, ed. (New York: Harper & Row, 1960), II: pp. 380–381. Herbert Marcuse understands Marxism as an heir to the Enlightenment tradition. He traces the roots of that tradition to the Radical Reformers, the medieval Cathari, and the ancient Gnostics. See Herbert Marcuse, *Soviet Marxism* (London: Routledge & Kegan Paul, 1958), pp. 200–201.

8. Eric Voegelin, *The New Science of Politics* (Chicago: University of Chicago Press, 1952), p. 118. Many people seem to labor under the assumption that Voegelin is an orthodox Christian and a political conservative. To the contrary, he has told me candidly that he does not regard himself as either. Also see Karl Loewith, *Meaning in History* (Chicago: University of Chicago Press, 1949), pp. 103, 112–113, 160–173.

9. Robert C. Tucker, *Philosophy and Myth in Karl Marx* (London: Cambridge University Press, 1961), p. 31.

10. Kenneth Hamilton, *What's New in Religion?* (Grand Rapids: Eerdmans, 1968), p. 72.

11. Douglas J. Hall, "The Theology of Hope in an Officially Optimistic Society," *Religion in Life, XL* (Autumn 1971), p. 380.

12. *ON*, p. 98.

13. Roger Garaudy, *Karl Marx: The Evolution of His Thought* (New York: International, 1967), p. 205.

14. *ON*, p. 37.

15. Juergen Moltmann, "Hope without Faith: An Eschatological Humanism without God," *Is God Dead?*, Johannes B. Metz, ed. (New York: Paulist, 1966), p. 27. Italics added.

16. Roger Garaudy and Quentin Lauer, S.J., *A Christian-Communist*

Dialogue (Garden City, N. Y.: Doubleday, 1968), p. 69. Italics added.

17. E. L. Mascall, *The Secularization of Christianity* (New York: Holt, Rinehart and Winston, 1965), p. 7. Regarding those Christians who collapse heavenly transcendence into worldly (futurist) transcendence, Herbert Marcuse has said: "I am at a loss to say in what terms they are still Christian" [H. Marcuse (with Harvey Wheeler), "Varieties of Humanism," *The Center Magazine, I* (July 1968), p. 15].

18. Karl Barth, *Against the Stream* (London: SCM Press, 1954), p. 223.

19. Editorial, "Swedish Bishops Condemn Premarital Intercourse," *TCC, LXXXI* (June 24, 1964), p. 822. Copyright 1964 Christian Century Foundation. Reprinted by permission.

20. Henry Paolucci, ed., *The Political Writings of St. Augustine* (Chicago: Gateway, 1962), p. 332.

21. See Reinhold Niebuhr, *Christian Realism and Political Problems* (New York: Scribner's, 1953), pp. 122–123. Also see Galatians 5:19ff.

22. See *GR*, p. 16. Unfortunately, Cox neglects his own distinction.

23. Jacques Maritain, *The Peasant of the Garonne* (New York: Macmillan, 1968), pp. 75–76. For a classically Protestant view, see John Calvin, *On God and Political Duty* (Indianapolis: Bobbs-Merrill, 1956), pp. 31–43. For a contemporary Protestant statement of the same perspective, see Jacques Ellul, *False Presence of the Kingdom* (New York: Seabury, 1972). Also see I Timothy 4:4.

24. *SC*, p. 223.

25. See *ibid.*, pp. 127, 124, and *GR*, p. 27.

26. See *SS*, pp. 231, 235, 255. Religious liberals are characteristically "so lost in the relativities of history that every slight eminence in the landscape of time seems to be a final mountain peak of the Kingdom of God" [Reinhold Niebuhr, *Essays in Applied Christianity* (New York: Meridian, 1959), p. 149].

27. Quoted in Francine du Plessix Gray, *Divine Disobedience: Profiles in Catholic Radicalism* (New York: Vintage, 1969), p. 145. Also see Philip Berrigan, *No More Strangers* (New York: Macmillan, 1965), pp. 117–118. For a case study on how the Berrigans relate their politicized understanding of Providence and the Kingdom to conceptions of collective guilt, see Dale Vree, " 'Stripped Clean':

The Berrigans and the Politics of Guilt and Martyrdom," *Ethics, 85* (July 1975), pp. 271–287.

28. Philip Berrigan, *Prison Journals of a Priest Revolutionary* (New York: Ballantine, 1967), pp. 217–218.

29. Garry Wills, *Politics and Catholic Freedom* (Chicago: Regnery, 1964), p. 126.

30. For example, see *GR*, p. 31.

31. Walter Rauschenbusch, *Christianity and the Social Crisis* (New York: Harper & Row, 1969), pp. 339, 336.

32. Quoted in George Lichtheim, *The Concept of Ideology and Other Essays* (New York: Vintage, 1967), p. 108. Italics added.

33. Karl Barth, *The German Church Conflict* (Richmond: John Knox, 1965), p. 16. Italics added. Also see J. S. Conway, *The Nazi Persecution of the Churches: 1933–45* (New York: Basic Books, 1968), p. 11.

34. H. Richard Niebuhr, *The Kingdom of God in America* (New York: Harper & Row, 1937), p. 197.

35. Franklin H. Littell, "The Protestant Churches and Totalitarianism (Germany 1933–1945)," *Totalitarianism,* Carl J. Friedrich, ed. (New York: Universal Library, 1954), pp. 110–111.

36. Will Herberg, "Introduction—The Social Philosophy of Karl Barth," *Community, State and Church,* Karl Barth (Garden City, N. Y.: Anchor, 1960), p. 15.

37. See Charles C. West, *Communism and the Theologians* (New York: Macmillan, 1958), p. 67. A more ambiguous—and perhaps more intriguing—case is represented by one of Barth's major allies in the fight against the German-Christians, Joseph L. Hromádka, who came close to adopting Berecsky's stand on Communism. While Hromádka intimated that God had spoken through the Communist revolution in 1948 in his native Czechoslovakia, he avoided equating the Kingdom of God with man-made utopias and endowing Communism with an organic relation to the Christian hope. Regarding Hromádka, see *ibid.,* p. 74; Hromádka, *Impact of History on Theology* (Notre Dame, Ind.: Fides, 1970), p. 37; Hromádka, *Theology Between Yesterday and Tomorrow* (Philadelphia: Westminster, 1957), p. 51; Hromádka, "The Situation in Czechoslovakia," *The Religious Situation 1969,* Donald R. Cutler, ed. (Boston: Beacon, 1969), p. 59; West, "Josef Hromadka," *Mod-*

ern Theologians, Thomas E. Bird, ed. (Notre Dame, Ind.: University of Notre Dame Press, 1967), pp. 41, 51, 57, 59; Matthew Spinka, "Church in a Communist Society: A Study of J. L. Hromádka's Theological Politics," *The Hartford Seminary Foundation Bulletin,* No. 17 (June 1954), pp. 3, 36, 42; and Hans Ruh, *Geschichte und Theologie: Grundlinien der Theologie Hromadkas: Nachwort von J. L. Hromadka* (Zuerich: EVZ-Verlag, 1963), pp. 5–13, 36–47.

38. "Barth to Bereczky: A Letter," *TCC, LXIX* (July 30, 1952), p. 876.

39. Karl Loewith, *Meaning in History* (Chicago: University of Chicago Press, 1949), p. 196. Also see Abraham J. Heschel, *The Prophets* (New York: Harper & Row, 1962), 1: p. 176.

40. Jacques Lebreton, S. J. and Jacques Zeiller, *Heresy and Orthodoxy* (New York: Collier, 1946), p. 66.

41. R. A. Knox, *Enthusiasm* (Oxford: Oxford University Press, 1950), p. 37.

42. Jean Guitton, *Great Heresies and Church Councils* (New York: Harper & Row, 1965), p. 123.

43. See Paul Ramsey, *Who Speaks for the Church?* (New York: Abingdon, 1967), p. 167.

44. Letter to *TCC, LXXX* (May 15, 1963), p. 649.

45. Abraham J. Heschel, *The Prophets* (New York: Harper & Row, 1962), 1: p. 123. According to R. Niebuhr, "Micah was only one prophet among four hundred. Perhaps the percentage of pure prophecy is not much higher even today. . . ." [R. Niebuhr, *Beyond Tragedy* (New York: Scribner's, 1965), pp. 82–83]. There is a minoritarian, but not heretical, current in Christianity which interprets Old and New Testament prophecy "literally" and believes God is working through the political events of the day in preparation for the apocalyptic Second Coming of Christ. Here, Providence is manifest; however, these Christians do not set themselves up as new prophets with a new word from God on how to usher in the Kingdom; rather they simply interpret established prophecy. Most of them are nonpolitical and tend not to confuse Providence with their favorite political projects.

46. Niebuhr, *Beyond Tragedy,* p. 65. Italics added. Also see Heschel, *op. cit.,* p. xv.

47. Gerhard von Rad, *The Message of the Prophets* (London: SCM Press, 1968), p. 39. Also see pp. 46–47.

48. Seymour Martin Lipset and Richard B. Dobson, "The Intellectual as Critic and Rebel," *Daedalus, 101* (Summer 1972), p. 179.

49. Daniel Callahan, in *Spectrum of Catholic Attitudes,* Robert Campbell, O.P., ed. (Milwaukee: Bruce, 1969), pp. 175–176.

50. Niebuhr, *Beyond Tragedy,* p. 18.

51. Roger Garaudy, "What Does a Non-Christian Expect of the Church in Matters of Social Morality?" *The Social Message of the Gospels,* Franz Boekle, ed. (New York: Paulist, 1968), p. 35.

52. Herbert Aptheker, *The Urgency of Marxist-Christian Dialogue* (New York: Harper & Row, 1970), p. 72.

53. *ON,* p. ix. See *SS,* pp. 64 and 76 for a more guarded view.

54. *TH,* p. 22.

55. Garaudy, "We Are Struggling on Behalf of Man," *Political Affairs XLV* (July 1966), p. 23. Cox's and Moltmann's inversion of the concept of Original Sin is clearly endorsed by Garaudy: "The great fault—the sin—is . . . resignation. Sin is not the pride of wanting to be more than a man, it is the servility of agreeing to be less than a man." Garaudy, *Reconquête de l'espoir* (Paris: Grasset, 1971), pp. 118–119 (the translation is mine).

56. Martin D'Arcy, *Communism and Christianity* (Great Britain: Penguin, 1956), p. 80. Said R. Niebuhr: "The Kingdom of God, the final ideal, is always beyond history. What is in history is always partial to specific interests and tainted by sin" [R. Niebuhr, *Essays in Applied Christianity,* p. 160].

57. Karl Barth, *Community, State and Church,* p. 126. This same emphasis is found in the writings of Barth's disciple, Jacques Ellul.

58. Pope Paul VI, "Credo of the People of God," (pamphlet) (New York: Paulist, 1968), p. 35. It should *not* be thought that *all* dialogical Christians adhere to heretical eschatology (not to mention heretical views of Original Sin and revelation). For example, a leading dialogical Catholic, Karl Rahner, S.J., who is able to see a certain unspecifiable affinity between sacred and profane futures, has emphasized that the eschatological future, the sacred future, "is that to which we ourselves cannot reach out, but which rather comes to us of itself—when it decides to—and with which we have to deal, strangely, precisely on *these* terms. The future is that which does not evolve, that which is not planned, that which is not under our control. . . . The future is that which silently lies in

wait, and which, when it springs out upon us, rips up the nets of all our plans, the false 'future' which we ourselves have constructed . . . ." [K. Rahner, "A Fragmentary Aspect of a Theological Evaluation of the Concept of the Future," *Theological Investigations* (London: Darton, Longman & Todd, 1973), X: p. 237].

59. *New Catholic Encyclopedia* (1967), s.v. "Kingdom of God," by M. J. Cantley. Also see 1 Timothy 6:15, Acts 1:6–7, and 1 Thessalonians 5:1ff. For similar emphases coming from respected, but perhaps generally nonorthodox sources, see Norman Perrin, *The Kingdom of God in the Teaching of Jesus* (Philadelphia: Westminster, 1963), p. 52, and H. Richard Niebuhr, *The Kingdom of God in America* (New York: Harper & Row, 1937), pp. 191–193.

60. Oscar Cullmann, *The State in the New Testament* (New York: Scribner's, 1956), p. 9.

61. *Ibid.*, pp. 15–16. Curiously, some Gnostic writers have gone so far as to vindicate Judas Iscariot. See Walter Niggs, *The Heretics* (New York: Knopf, 1962), p. 35.

62. Cullmann, *op. cit.*, p. 21.

63. Cullmann, *Jesus and the Revolutionaries* (New York: Harper & Row, 1970), p. 13. The opposite point of view on Jesus' relation to the Zealot movement can be found in the works of Karl Kautsky, S. G. F. Brandon, and others. My citation of Cullmann is intended to illustrate the orthodox view, not as a judgment on a scholarly dispute.

64. George Eldon Ladd, *The Presence of the Future,* rev. ed. of *Jesus and the Kingdom* (Grand Rapids: Eerdmans, 1974), p. 3. Also see Perrin, *op. cit.*, pp. 57, 79, 158–159. This consensus is in the realm of biblical scholarship, not necessarily in the realm of systematic theology or social ethics.

65. Ladd, *op. cit.*, p. 204.

66. *Ibid.*, pp. 159, 333. Although the eschatological future is built *by* God, *when* he chooses, there are various opinions among the orthodox on the question of whether the acts of men will be destroyed or merely "transformed" (hence, in some sense, survive) in the Eschaton. If the latter option is favored, then it is possible that historical human actions are not utterly and entirely irrelevant to the Eschaton, although very little, if anything, can be said regarding either the *extent* of the relevance, or the *way* in

which certain human accomplishments will be transformed and perfected by God's grace. Regarding this transformation option, see Ellul, *op. cit.,* pp. 19–26; *Second Vatican Council: Pastoral Constitution on the Church in the Modern World* [Gaudium et Spes] (Washington, D.C.: National Catholic Welfare Conference, 1966); and Rahner, "The Theological Problems Entailed in the Idea of the 'New Earth,'" *op. cit.,* X: pp. 260–272.

3
Dialogical Christianity and Its Precedents

Beware of false prophets . . . .

MATTHEW 7:15 NEB

MODERN GNOSTICISM: THE ESSENCE OF DIALOGICAL CHRISTIANITY

Gnosticism was a prevalent religious mood in the ancient world and during the period when Christianity was born. Gnosticism did not manifest itself as an organized church with a codified set of beliefs. Although its many variations did derive from certain basic ideas, it was essentially eclectic and syncretistic. It often existed as a parasite on the body of other religions. Within Christianity, Christian Gnostics challenged the Church Fathers. It was in opposition to this heretical tendency that the Church began to define itself by formalizing the scriptural canon, codifying the liturgy, emphasizing the Apostolic episcopate and tradition as vehicles of orthodox authority, and formulating the creeds. The very way in which the Church defined itself constituted an emphatic condemnation of Gnosticism.

The essence of Gnosticism was a revolt against the Old Testament God of creation as well as against the created order itself. The Gnostics regarded creation and the world as unambiguously evil. Therefore, the God who was responsible for this creation must himself be evil. It can be seen how Gnosticism was an inversion of Christianity, which regarded the world *(kosmos)* and the body as fundamentally good, and the God of creation as absolutely good. The Gnostics posited a God above the evil creator-God. The God of the Gnostics was an alien, good, and transmundane God who had virtually nothing to do with this evil world. In the Gnostic scheme, matter is evil and spirit good. Because of this dichotomy, Gnosticism was (and is) radically dualistic.

Gnosticism was an eschatological religion of salvation—salvation not from sin, but from the material world. It taught that in their unregenerate state, men were asleep, drunken with this world, and ignorant. However, within their souls, all men possessed a "spark" of the divine, the *gnōsis,* the knowledge which effects salvation. The prophet or messenger from the alien God called men out of their sleep into true knowledge. At death the soul ascended out of this world to be reunited with the divinity. Through time, as all of these portions of the divine are gathered in, the divinity was to be reunited in itself and find fulfillment.

According to Gnostic symbolism, the Devil was the first messenger from the alien God. When he induced Adam and Eve to eat of the tree of knowledge, *gnōsis* first entered the world, constituting the first successful rebellion against the evil creator-God. This inversion of the conventional symbols of good and evil, says Hans Jonas, is typical of the "heretical method."[1] Likewise, the Gnostics regarded Prometheus as a hero. He had scorned Zeus, the god of this world, in the name of the good God beyond this world. (In Chapter 4, I note how Marxian atheism is built on a fealty to the Promethean heritage. Dialogical Christians, in seeking points of contact with Marxists, have adopted Prometheus as a hero. It will be revealing to see— below—what then happens to their professed faith in the Hebrew-Christian creator-God.)

Modern Gnosticism differs from the ancient variety in that it dispenses with the alien "God above God" as well as with the creator-God. According to Thomas J. J. Altizer, modern Gnosticism is the "search for an authentic redemption from an alien cosmos in the context of the death of God."[2] Nevertheless, it retains the notion that man contains within himself a divine spark of sorts, that man in his essence is possessed of original innocence and purity. The present condition of the world is still evil, and man is essentially good and potentially godlike. When the present world is overturned, the divine sparks will be gathered together, so to speak, and man will be able to realize his divine nature. Gnosticism's radical world-denial is transformed from a spatial to a temporal dimension. The state of fulfillment is no longer in another world after death, but rather is projected into an earthly future. In keeping with the messianism of our times, modern Gnosticism is radically future-oriented.

Modern Gnosticism still regards the present world as wholly evil; however, the word "present" must be emphasized. The world *(kosmos)* is rejected in the name of a totally transfigured world. By "world" here is understood primarily the social, economic, and political structures and secondarily the reactionary ideological, philosophical, and ethical configurations. Salvation is total revolution, ushering in the utopia of a new earth.

There is a sense, however, in which the world (as *aiōn*) is good. The Spirit of the Age is the agency of salvation. The Zeitgeist (in conjunction with its manifestation as *gnōsis* in the psyche of the enlightened ones) carries the potential of a totally reconstituted *kosmos*. Once the weary old *kosmos* is revolutionized, the immanental divine sparks are gathered together. Then the Zeitgeist finds self-fulfillment, and man and society are divinized.

For Marxists, the *gnōsis* is the Marxist ideology itself. Armed with the *gnōsis,* Marxists have privileged insight into the necessitarian workings of matter. Matter itself acquires metaphysical qualities and manifests "all the attributes of Hegel's Absolute."[3] The Zeitgeist operates in both the *gnōsis* possessed by the revolutionary elect and in the metaphysical movements of matter.

For dialogical Christians, the *gnōsis* is usually a quasi-Marxist ideology of some kind. The Zeitgeist is confounded with the Holy Spirit or the providential working of a "politician-God," both of which in turn are largely defined in terms of the imperatives of the Enlightenment and Marxism. The central symbol is the earthly New Jerusalem—built by man in cooperation with a benevolent Spirit of the Age—which is the equivalent of Marxism's classless society.

According to Eric Voegelin, pre-Christian society was polytheistic, hence divinized. With the rise of Christianity, existence was divided into a sacred realm (heaven and the Church) and a secular or temporal realm (society and politics, etc.).[4] But, added Voegelin, "Uncertainty is the very essence of Christianity. The feeling of security in a 'world full of gods' is lost with the gods themselves; when the world is de-divinized, communication with the world-transcendent God is reduced to the tenuous bond of faith. . . ." However, "the very lightness of this fabric may prove too heavy a burden for men who lust for massively possessive experience."[5] With this fall from faith, man must be able to fall back on something else, something more imposing yet "sufficiently close to the experience of faith that only a discerning eye would see the difference. . . ."[6] An alternative was found in the hydralike phenomenon that dogged Christianity from its very inception—Gnosticism.

The result in modern times has been—from the orthodox Christian viewpoint—a fallacious immanentization of the Christian Eschaton whereby man seeks to inject ultimate meaning into secular history. But from the orthodox point of view, there is no such meaning in secular history, only in sacred history— which culminates in the Eschaton. "The attempt at immanentizing the meaning of existence is fundamentally an attempt at bringing our knowledge of transcendence into a firmer grip than the *cognitio fidei,* the cognition of faith, will afford; and Gnostic experiences offer this firmer grip. . . ."[7] These experiences permit the redivinization of society and the divinization of man. This effort at self-salvation is characteristic of modern civilization; hence, Voegelin understands "the essence of modernity as the growth of gnosticism."[8]

It is clear that Marxist messianism is atheistic. However, from the orthodox Christian vantage point, it would seem that any kind of political messianism, regardless of how much God-talk is thrown in, must necessarily be atheistic in effect. Orthodox Christianity has always insisted that the messianic Kingdom of God is necessarily an act of God, not man. Any effort to establish the Kingdom by man's own might is heretical—it is a usurpation of God's prerogative, an attempt to seize what belongs only to God. Hence, the words of the dialogical Marxist, Ernst Bloch, are pregnant with meaning: "The existence of God— indeed God as such, as a distinct being—is superstition; faith is solely the belief in a messianic kingdom of God, without God. Therefore, far from being an enemy of religious utopianism, atheism is its premiss [sic]: *without atheism there is no room for messianism.*"[9] At first this sounds puzzling. But there *is* something atheistic about heretical eschatology—indeed (as Bloch mentions later), there is a certain Promethean hubris involved in this heretical *self-injection* into God or transcendence. By not waiting on God, the heretics are in effect denying him. This utopian compulsion to inject oneself into the Godhead or transcendence is characteristic of the Gnostic Christianity of Joachim di Fiore and Thomas Muentzer (to be discussed below) as well as that of many dialogical Christians.

Since "there is no passage in the New Testament from which advice for revolutionary political action could be extracted . . . ,"[10] Gnosticism requires a second source of revelation to justify self-injection into the Eschaton. Ancient Gnostics tended to reject the Old Testament outright and were highly selective and frequently allegorical in their approach to the New. Consequently, in Montanist fashion, they stressed the superiority of immediate and direct revelations to the individual, as well as secret traditions and secret gospels (neither known to the Church nor part of its Scriptures) as new sources of revelation. With the licensing of such subjective sources of revelation, it was easy to find justifications for self-injection into the Eschaton. Furthermore, because the doctrine of Original Sin seems to deny man the capacity to establish a perfect society, that doctrine must either be denied or seriously qualified. In this regard it is worth noting again that there is no place for Original Sin in Gnosticism (ancient or modern). This puts Gnosticism in diametrical opposition to Christianity—which holds that man's innate, but willful, proclivity to sin is the source of evil in the world. The world is essentially good whereas man is sinful (just as the body is essentially good whereas the soul or heart is corrupt). Gnosticism holds that the world is evil whereas man (in his soul) is good, the body is evil but the soul good. Gnosticism locates the source of evil in the creation, in the structures

of the world, in man's environment. Gnostic salvation has nothing to do with the remission of sin, since sin is not at issue. The
problem is not sin, but man's ignorance. Hence, the remedy is
not *faith* (in God's mercy and grace), but *gnōsis* (literally,
knowledge). Salvation is not the result of this forgiveness of
sins; it is found in that enlightenment which liberates one from
creatureliness, from contamination with the world. Enlightenment opens the door to self-deification.

Christ's Atonement for sin is irrelevant to the Gnostic. Man is
not a sinner, he is not a perpetrator of evil; rather, he is a *victim*
of an evil world. Therefore, the Gnostics regarded Adam not as
a sinner, but as the victim of persecution by the rulers of this
world. Said Jonas: "Here is one simple criterion for what is
'Christian' (orthodox) or 'gnostic' (heretical): whether the guilt
is Adam's or the Archon's [the rulers of this world, or simply the
world]. . . . The difference goes to the heart of the gnostic
problem."[11]

In summary, from an orthodox standpoint, modern Gnosticism (like modern gnosticized Christianity) is a heretical form
of Christianity which requires: (1) a second source of revelation, (2) a denial of Original Sin, and (3) a view of the Kingdom
as established by man's efforts. Just as the essence of modernity
is Gnostic, likewise the essence of modern dialogical Christianity is Gnostic. As we shall see, Harvey Cox and Juergen Moltmann are essentially modern Gnostics (although not every element in their thought can be construed as Gnostic).

THE PRECEDENT IN JOACHIM DI FIORE AND THOMAS MUENTZER

The early Christians expected an imminent end of the world
and the establishment of the Kingdom of God on earth as a
millennium wherein Christ and his saints would rule. It was to
be terminated by the Day of Judgment, on which it would be

revealed who would enter heaven and who hell. As it became clear that the millennium was not imminent, the Church began to reinterpret its understanding of the Kingdom. St. Augustine gave definitive form to this reinterpretation. In place of the premillennial view, he substituted the amillennial view, which generally held that the millennial Kingdom is realized on earth within the community of believers or the Church itself. The Church persists in history until the Day of Judgment when the Kingdom is fulfilled.

The Augustinian position, however, has met with various forms of resistance (many of them heretical) throughout church history. Around A.D. 1000 there was much excitement about the imminent end of the world. The resistance to Augustinian eschatology came to a head in the person and teaching of the Cistercian monk from Calabria in Italy, Joachim di Fiore (1132–1202). In Joachim Gnostic and Montanist tendencies blossomed.

In opposition to Augustine, who had separated reality into the sacred and the profane, Joachim sought the redivinization of earthly existence. He saw profane history as a gradual ascent to perfection. As Ernst Benz said: "Joachim is the first theologian of history who introduced the idea of progress into the theology of history."[12]

Joachim superimposed the symbolism of the Trinity onto historical development. Hence, there were three stages to history. The first was the Age of the Father, an age of law and fear; the second was the Age of the Son, an age of the Gospel; the third was the Age of the Holy Spirit, an age of total freedom, angelic perfection, and communal bliss. Joachim predicted that the Third Age would begin in 1260. The eruption of the Third Age would be abrupt and apocalyptic (yet it would also be in a sense the culmination point of a gradual process of maturation). He regarded the church as the Antichrist, as wholly corrupt (a view which surfaced again among the sectarian Radicals during the Reformation), so that the Third Age could not be ushered in until the church had been totally destroyed.

Joachim claimed an illumination he received directly from the Holy Spirit as authority for his prophecies and theological speculations. But since there is no transparent justification in the Bible or church tradition for his teaching of the Third Age, an orthodox Christian would have been inclined to regard his revelation as bogus. Since the world was not in fact transformed in or around 1260, that inclination would seem to be vindicated.

It was characteristic of Joachim and the entire Joachite tradition to subordinate the Bible and church to the free-form illuminations of the Holy Spirit. This was certainly a Montanist unitarianism of the Third Person. It is not surprising, then, that there was little place for Christ in Joachim's thinking. Said Norman Cohn: "Christ no longer stands at the centre of history and the Christian revelation is of only limited and temporary validity."[13] In the crisp words of Bloch, "He . . . dissolved Christ in a commune." Nor was there place for God the Father. Said Bloch: "He deposed the theology of the Father, [and] relegated it to the age of fear and servitude. . . ."[14]

The Third Age was to be initiated by the Holy Spirit. In it there would be a voluntary and communal poverty. There would be no need for the church, the sacraments, or even the Scriptures. The validity of all these would be superseded by a higher spiritual understanding, for indeed carnal bodies would be exchanged for spiritual bodies requiring no food for sustenance. The heart of these spiritual beings would be illumined directly by the Holy Spirit.

There is a striking congruence between the method of Joachim's theological speculation and the Third Age itself. For both, there is an exclusive reliance on the Holy Spirit. In both, the authority of the Bible, the church, God, and Christ are neutralized. In fact, what has been constructed is a second revelation, a *gnōsis*, imparted directly to the heart of the elect by the Spirit. However, this Spirit is the functional equivalent of the Gnostic "God above God," since God the Father and God the Son have become superfluous anachronisms.

Like all ancient Gnostics, Joachim regarded matter as evil and spirit as good. He abhorred the order of creation (the *kosmos*) and sought release through intense spiritualization. He had little regard for Christ's Incarnation in the flesh, or for the tradition and sacraments of the Catholic Church.

He lusted after a "massively possessive experience" (to recall Voegelin's words) by means of an overwhelming illumination from the Holy Spirit. He sought to imbue profane history with transcendental meaning and purpose, and to immanentize the Eschaton by calling forth a Third Age of the Holy Spirit. In the words of Bloch, "He was the first to set a date for the kingdom of God, for the communist kingdom, and to demand its observance."[15]

He did not seek to construct the Third Age by human powers. Although he prophesied its arrival at a certain date, he expected its arrival to be effected by a supernatural agency. Nevertheless, there was a "certain inner logic" in his position which demanded that one anticipate the future by preparing for the transformation oneself.[16] This tendency came to the fore in many of his disciples, and particularly in Thomas Muentzer, who sought to seize the Kingdom by force.

Joachim is a pivotal figure in the history of the West. He broke the grip which the Augustinian view of history had upon the Western mind. He cracked the dikes which the Catholic Church had so assiduously built up over the previous centuries against the tempestuous seas of enthusiasm (from *entheos*, the divinity within; hence, free-form religious excitement unchecked by scriptural or ecclesiastical authority). He inspired countless heretics who followed him and took his ideas and methods to their logical conclusion. He was a precursor to the secular messianic movements of modernity. According to Benz, "By joining the ideas of progress and development with the prophecy of the imminent fulfillment of the history of salvation, Joachim has created the model for the religious, social, political, and philosophical utopias of modern times."[17] According to Voegelin, Joachim "created the aggregate of symbols which govern the self-interpretation of modernity to this day,"[18] namely: (1) the periodization of history into three stages, (2) the charismatic leader, (3) the prophet or intellectual, and (4) the brotherhood of autonomous persons or utopia. Cohn said that Joachim's influence has been indirect but long-term and immense, and can be seen "most clearly in those latter-day 'philosophies of history' which are most emphatically anti-Christian."[19] As examples, he cited Auguste Comte, who divided history into three stages (the theological, the metaphysical, and the scientific); Karl Marx, who also divided history into three stages (primitive communism, class society, and fullblown communism); and the National Socialist fantasies of a Third Reich which would last a thousand years. In addition to these, Karl Loewith saw Joachim's influence in Lessing, the Saint-Simonian socialists, Hegel, and Schelling.[20] Curiously, in Charles Reich's recent pop speculations, the utopian age will be ushered in by those people illumined by Consciousness *III*.[21]

In Germany during the Reformation the Joachite tradition was carried on by Thomas Muentzer (ca. 1488–1525), the leader of the revolutionary wing of the Radical Reformation (as opposed to the mainstream or Magisterial Reformation of Luther and Calvin). The urge to seize the Third Age by coercive human action, which was implicit in Joachim, became explicit in Muentzer (also spelled Muenzer). Although there is no direct evidence that Muentzer regarded himself as a disciple of Joachim, Abraham Friesen has allowed that "Muentzer's ideology was influenced by Joachist thought, or, at the very least, ran along similar lines."[22] The same Gnostic and Montanist tendencies found in Joachim are found in Muentzer—but in exacerbated and revolutionary form.

Like Montanus and Joachim, Muentzer gave primacy to the inspiration of the Holy Spirit over all other authorities. As such, he set himself against the Reformation of Martin Luther as well as against the Catholic Church. The Spirit is not mediated to man through such externals as the Bible, tradition, or the sacraments; rather the Spirit is received directly into one's heart. The Bible's authority is spiritual, not literal, for it is only a record of how the Spirit moved in apostolic times. However, Muentzer felt he was living in the Last Days, and the Spirit was communicating directly with his chosen people; therefore what had been revealed in apostolic times was being superseded. To be possessed of the Spirit, Muentzer felt, was to become perfect, even godlike, and to be licensed to construct the Kingdom of God on earth. Engels himself interpreted this Promethean snatching of the stuff of divinity out of heaven as heretical, even atheistic: "His theologic-philosophic doctrine attacked all the main points not only of Catholicism but of Christianity as such. Under the cloak of Christian forms, he preached a kind of pantheism . . . and at times even taught open atheism. He repudiated the assertion that the Bible was the only infallible revelation. The only living revelation, he said, was reason [and] . . . the Holy Spirit was our reason."[23] Muentzer's Spirit was clearly a second source of revelation. Hence, it is no surprise that Luther (not to mention the Catholic Church) regarded Muentzer as a false prophet.

It was characteristic of the Radical Reformers to insist that one could not be *born* into Christianity. Instead, one could only become a Christian after going through a conversion experience as an adult. Hence, they demanded adult baptism in place of infant baptism. They did not accept the validity of infant baptism as practiced by the Catholics, Lutherans, or Calvinists. To join one of the Radical sects one had to be rebaptized. Hence, Radical Reformers were known as "Anabaptists," or rebaptizers. Although Muentzer was not typical of generic Anabaptism on every point, he did insist on adult baptism and the adult conversion experience. On the question of conversion, Muentzer rejected the Lutheran emphasis on justification by faith alone, and in its place he elaborated a theology of suffering whereby one could not be converted unless one had mortified one's flesh. To be a Christian required more than faith. One must be "daily conscious of the [fresh] revelation of God," one must hear the "inner Word" in the depths of one's soul. But to receive a direct revelation from God or the Holy Spirit, Muentzer taught that one must first expect to undergo "painful tribulation."[24] Through the experience of pain and suffering— the mortification of the flesh—the Holy Spirit is enabled to purify the soul, thereby preparing it for a fresh revelation.

Muentzer had been influenced by the mystic Johannes Tauler who understood the Bible allegorically and taught that "one must overcome the 'darkness of the flesh' by searching for the God who is already within man in the 'divine spark,' and by attaining complete 'independence from creatureliness'. . . ."[25] This is all markedly Gnostic, for Gnostics typically believe that creatureliness causes sin rather than vice versa (as the orthodox believe). Hence, salvation comes through the transcendence of creatureliness, in particular, self-deification, rather than through the remission of sins granted by the Atonement. For the orthodox, the quest of self-deification is of course the quintessence of Original Sin; indeed, it is the "original" sin of Adam and Eve. Luther probably recognized this Gnostic twist when he said of Muentzer: "he boasted how he had changed and slain his physical nature. This was indeed a really fanatical *(schwaermerisch)* statement. . . . For God wills that physical nature should be sustained and not extinguished."[26]

Any Gnostic would be unable to accept the Incarnation of God in Christ and Christ's Atonement on the cross, two of Christianity's cardinal doctrines. Since the flesh is regarded as evil it is inconceivable to the Gnostic that any good and true God would choose to be incarnated in human flesh—such would be an unspeakable profanation. Thus, Gnosticism usually entails a Docetic Christology. Moreover, since Original Sin is not a Gnostic belief it would be hard to know what to make of the Atonement. It is in terms of this issue of sin and atonement that Muentzer's political and military activism can best be comprehended.

In typically Gnostic fashion, Muentzer denied the historical Christ, the Jesus of flesh and blood, and substituted a dehistoricized, spiritual Christ. Muentzer's spiritualized Christ was not the Christ of traditional Christianity. His Christ was not the Second Person of the Trinity, but merely a derivative aspect of the Holy Spirit (which was for Muentzer the equivalent of the Gnostic "God above God"). In this way he was able to get around the doctrine of the Atonement (not to mention the Incarnation). Said Eric W. Gritsch: "The cross, then, is no longer the experience of the historical Jesus of Nazareth, who effected salvation through his historical death, but a spiritual experience, mediated through the Holy Spirit."[27] Christ's alleged suffering, therefore, had no substitutionary or sacrificial power because Christ did not *really* suffer on the cross for man's sins. Man was left by Muentzer to atone for his own sins—hence, the imperative to suffer, to slay one's own flesh. Every person had to earn his own salvation by repeating the suffering of Christ. However, such suffering was deemed insufficient to redeem the whole world. The world could be redeemed only when one further step was taken, namely, when all evil was positively extinguished.

There was a problem here, however, for what was to be done with the godless Catholics and Magisterial Protestants who refused perfection through the mortification of the flesh and the supposed indwelling of the Spirit, who refused to revolutionize the church, and who therefore perpetuated the evil world and frustrated the millennial fulfillment? The solution was implicit in Muentzerian theology. Once the flesh had been mortified and the Spirit had illumined the heart, the believer became one of a select group of perfect beings; in fact he became divine. As a god (or part of God), he quite literally had license to do whatever he deemed right. The Muentzerian need not answer to any Bible, church, or code of ethics. He was an autonomous man, a superman. In his quest for immediate salvation, for the redivinization of the world, he could use any method he wanted, for— in antinomian fashion—he was beyond "good" and "evil."

Muentzer regarded himself as a prophetic messianic leader. He felt authorized to inflict pain and suffering (mortification) on the godless recalcitrants—for their own good, one must presume. But if they persisted in their godlessness, they deserved extermination. In fact, Muentzer set up his own secret military vanguard, the League of the Elect, to execute his redemptive mandate. The millennial Kingdom was, by definition, a state of perfection. The godless had no right to impede the coming Kingdom, they had no right to life. Armed with this theology, Muentzer set out to establish the New Jerusalem with violence.

Muentzer's chiliasm is emphatically heretical because Christian orthodoxy insists that when the Kingdom comes in its fullness, it will come as an act of God. Because of the clarity with which the orthodox position has been maintained throughout history, almost all heretical chiliasts at least pay what appears to be lip service to it. Even Muentzer did. However, Muentzer thought it was possible to force God's hand, to oblige him to act. It was this kind of rationalization that freed Muentzer's hands for action of his own. Whether he really believed God would intervene miraculously is dubious, but unimportant. We will see this kind of lip service also in Cox and Moltmann (where it gives rise to considerable confusion). The important point is that human action in the construction of the Kingdom derives from the heretical chiliastic understanding of the relation of man to God. In contrast to orthodoxy, which holds that man is subordinate to God and can in no way save himself, heretical chiliasm tends to either immanentize God or deify man—or both. Also, the distinction between profane and sacred history is usually blurred. God and man are seen as equals, as partners, as co-workers. The sovereign distinctiveness of God gets lost in the equation, so that it becomes impossible (hence ultimately irrelevant) to distinguish God's action from man's. For all intents and purposes, it is man who is constructing the Kingdom. The primary importance of human action is apparent in Muentzer's sermon to the princes, where he said: "Now if you want to be true governors, you must . . . as Christ commanded, drive his enemies from the elect. For you are the means to this end. Beloved, don't give us any old jokes about how the power of God should do it without your application of the sword. . . . God is your protection. . . . He will make your hands skilled in fighting and will also sustain you." This assurance of divine protection is itself dependent on human action, for it "cannot happen without suffering."[28]

From the point of view of many Marxists, Muentzer represents one of the clearest examples of what Christianity ought to be. According to Garaudy, "In Muenzer's militant millenarianism, Christians did not stop at an expectation of the kingdom, but proceeded to fight for it. . . . Here faith is no longer an opium. . . ."[29] Quite understandably, then, dialogical Christians, in searching for congruence with Marxism, have turned to Muentzer as something of a precedent for their own theorizing. This is no doubt a source of much of their heterodoxy.

HARVEY COX

Harvey Cox is probably the most influential Protestant theologian living in America today.[30] Within American Protestant theology, Cox has played a central role in the breakup of neo-orthodoxy. Michael Novak once pointed to the importance of Cox's work by referring to him as the Reinhold Niebuhr of the present generation.[31]

Cox is a Professor of Church and Society at the Harvard Divinity School. He has been a leading member of the Americans for Democratic Action, politically supportive of the New Left and the New Politics, a McGovern booster, and an admirer of Castro's Cuba.

Cox is an idiosyncratic American Baptist who has strong affinities with the politically-minded Anabaptists of the Radical Reformation. Martin E. Marty described him most aptly as a "Baptist Sectarian Utopian," a label Cox gladly accepts.[32] This is a way of saying he is more typical of the sometimes heretical Anabaptists than of the orthodox Baptists (even though there are historical links between the two).

Although Cox is not necessarily an "original thinker" in the purest sense of the term, his importance should not be underestimated. He is a superb synthesizer and popularizer—indeed, more of a pastoral, than a systematic, theologian. He is intellectually exciting, never dull or pedestrian. He has the ability to take current ideas from many sources and put them together into a distinctive and persuasive package. He has been a pioneer of the Marxist-Christian dialogue, and more than anyone else, his thought has epitomized the Christian contribution and response to the dialogue.

Even though sequential consistency is not one of his virtues, his overall thought manifests a continuity that superficial Cox-critics have failed to notice. (Unless noted, I shall treat his thought as a whole.) In 1965 he wrote a best-seller, *The Secular City*, which has frequently been hailed as one of the most significant books produced by a theologian in this century. It argued the case for a secular theology. One of the issues that inspired the writing of this book—which has sold more than 900,000 copies and gone through fourteen translations—was "how to affirm socialism and remain Christian at the same time."[33] Garaudy has said that its theology "seems to me the theology which is best suited to profound dialogue with Marxism."[34] In his later writings Cox comes to articulate a theology of hope and fantasy and modifies his thinking somewhat; however, these changes are minor compared to the fact that his thought continues to be basically secular and political, and abundantly amenable to dialogue with Marxism.

Cox places himself squarely in the tradition of the heretical and chiliastic sectarians of old: "I believe that the sectarian contribution must now be restated. . . . Some sectarians withdrew from the political realm, some became quietists, but the sectarians who interest me were those who wanted the reformation to change the society, not just the church."[35] He generally identifies with the tradition of Joachim and Muentzer (for which Marxists have shown great respect).[36] This has prompted Novak to say: "In American theological thought, Harvey Cox stands more nearly than any other in this [heretical and sectarian] tradition. It is not surprising, then, that Cox is the Christian theologian most sensitively attuned to the Christian-Marxist dialogue and the importance of the category of the future."[37]

Cox's attitude toward heresy is significant. He has proclaimed that the category of heresy is "virtually useless" because it "presumes that we already have the truth in our grasp. . . ."[38] He has exclaimed, "Let the apostate, the miscreant and the dissenter thrive!"[39] As such, he has called for a renewed appreciation of mania or madness, suggesting that some forms of madness are divine: "We must listen to the deviants of our society before pronouncing them all kooks. Some of them are. Some may be full of god. . . ."[40] But how is pneumatic madness to be distinguished from kooky madness? How is one to discern the spirits? To cope with these questions Cox will find that the category of heresy is far from useless; indeed, he will have to make use of some new standard of heresy and orthodoxy.

Aware of this need, Cox responds that whatever contributes to human liberation is truly of God. Indeed, liberation is the criterion of truth in every aspect of religion: "No matter how neatly a present rite or teaching may cohere with an orthodox past, if it locks people in stupefied bondage it . . . is 'heretical.' "[41] In fact, this standard is so absolute and universal that it even applies to non-Christian religions, certain aspects of which are liberating, hence true. Therefore, while Cox rejects the traditional Christian standard of orthodoxy and heresy for presuming to have the truth already in its grasp, he turns right around and establishes his own standard of truth, a standard entirely in step with the Spirit of the Age. He is even willing to speculate that perhaps it is the orthodox Christians who are the real heretics.[42]

Cox embodies the three basic heresies we have discussed up to this point. (1) There is apparently no fixed place for Original Sin in Cox's theology. Cox's God is a humanistic God who calls man to freedom, responsibility, and to the control of the natural and social environment. Such a God has not stacked the cards against man as fate did in Greek tragedy. Cox says that "man not only *should* but *can* 'have dominion over the earth.' For the Bible, there are no powers anywhere which are not essentially tameable and ultimately humanizable."[43] Cox takes the view that Original Sin is no impediment to man's ability to master the world; in fact, he regards the Resurrection as the event that marked the dissolution of the power of Original Sin over man's Promethean ambitions: "God deals with Adam's mixture of despair and egomania not by depriving him of his powers but by restoring them in the Second Adam [Jesus and his Resurrection]." According to this novel view, mankind has been liberated from "sin" ("understood as whatever chains people to the past") and "death" ("whatever terrifies them about the future").[44] Indeed, only if man is released from the bondage of Original Sin, only if the cards are not stacked against him, is he free and able to tame the powers that challenge his ascent. To be sure, Cox recognizes that evil has not yet been completely checked in the world today. But when looking to the future and proudly celebrating man's seemingly limitless ability to overcome the powers and mold the world to his own liking, Cox does not manifest the generally orthodox awareness of the provisional and finite nature of all human undertakings. This is strange for a Christian, for as Reinhold Niebuhr has said, "According to the Christian faith the pride, which seeks to hide the conditioned and finite character of all human endeavor, is the very quintessence of sin."[45] Cox, as noted above (on page 36), regards sloth, more than pride, as the quintessential sin (although he makes no attempt to construe sloth as an "original" sin which shackles human ambitions).

With such an unorthodox view of sin and evil, it is quite natural that (2) the building of the Kingdom of God on earth by human effort is a central edifice in Cox's thought. He seeks "the translation of the vision of the Kingdom of God into a vision of what we should strive and work and pray for on this earth, in this world. We're talking about the transformation of the kingdoms of the world into the kingdom of our God and of his Christ, and *I take this very literally.* . . ."[46]

In his earlier period, he identified the coming of the Kingdom with his own concept of the secular city. He held that the secular city was "a viable concretization of the ancient symbol of the Kingdom of God" and that "in the secular city itself we can discern certain provisional elements of the promised Kingdom."[47] As was pointed out above (on page 25), Cox was quite willing to be specific about when and where the Kingdom was breaking in.

The secular city consisted of two essentially irrevocable forces working in the modern world: urbanization and secularization. Cox contrived a neologism for the secular metropolis: technopolis. The technopolis creates a new cultural style out of the fusion of technology (techno-) and politics (-polis). In Joachite fashion, he divided human history into three epochs (that of tribe, town, and technopolis) and boldly declared that the technopolitan style is the wave of the future. The tribal epoch is characterized by magical primitive religion, the town epoch by metaphysical religion, and the technopolitan epoch by religionlessness and this-worldliness. Strangely, even though Cox emphasizes human freedom and autonomy, the realization of the secular city is an irrevocable process, immune from human desires.

Secularization is a constant theme in Cox's thought. It is associated in his mind with the coming Kingdom. It is "the loosing of the world from religious and quasi-religious understandings of itself, the dispelling of all closed worldviews, the breaking of all supernatural myths and sacred symbols. . . . Secularization occurs when man turns his attention away from worlds beyond and toward this world and this time (*saeculum*='this present age')."[48] Although Cox consistently invokes the "sacred symbol" of the Kingdom of God, and although the later Cox affirms such trappings of religion as mystery, ritual, myth, and cultic practices, the substance of his theology is and remains thoroughly secular—that is, it is oriented exclusively to this present age. He continues to disavow a supernatural God, miracles, metaphysics, and life after death. Whereas the earlier Cox identified the Kingdom with aspects of the secular city, the later Cox gives it a greater future dimension by identifying it with secular political fantasies and utopias, and with social self-transcendence in general. But he continues to identify the Kingdom with the fruits of secularization, which is a process of man's "coming of age" (a concept borrowed from Dietrich Bonhoeffer), man's maturation and assumption of responsibility for himself and his surroundings. In the process of secularization, "God is ever at work making freedom and personhood possible."[49]

Finally (3) as suggested above (on pages 24–26), Cox's God is the Zeitgeist. Cox advances the notion of a "politician-God" active in the secular world. This God is not to be thought of as supernatural: "I would say that God is pre-eminently and ultimately natural, that he works in, with, and under the natural processes of history, of nature. . . ."[50] Cox refuses to bifurcate reality into supernatural and secular realms; he refuses to vest God with supernatural attributes. What he offers us is a secular God to match the secular humanity he is offering us. Nevertheless, this God does act; in fact, he works manifestly (though not miraculously) in secular history, helping people realize the Promethean mandates of the Spirit of the Age. It is this secular God which functions as Cox's second source of revelation.

At issue in the Marxist-Christian dialogue is whether the Spirit of the Age (referred to as "God" or the "Holy Spirit" by dialogical Christians) is in some way an active ontological force that has its own initiative, or merely a passive collection of ideas and imperatives that does not interfere with human initiative. The central question is whether man is an autonomous or heteronomous being, whether Christianity allows people to be truly free, to determine the undetermined. Although Cox has liberated man from Original Sin and given him a decisive role to play in building the Kingdom, Cox retains the notion of God—thus arousing one's suspicion that people are not entirely free.

The issue of human autonomy is vital to both Christians and Marxists. Christians have repeatedly charged that Marxism is not humanistic because it subordinates man to the inexorable laws of history. These laws may be ultimately benign and guarantee man's success, but they deny man his freedom. Christians have argued that if the price of utopia is the loss of human freedom, then the price is too high. However, Marxists have been able to throw this argument back in the face of the Christians. As Bloch said: "Where there is a great master of the world there is no room for freedom, not even for the freedom of God's children."[51] From the moment of creation man is subordinate to and dependent upon God. Christianity has stressed that man can do nothing to save himself. The God of Christianity is a benevolent tyrant at best. Man may be free to go to hell, but to go to heaven, to achieve salvation, he must submit to God, he must renounce his freedom to do whatever he chooses. Marxists have claimed that this is too high a price to pay for salvation. Even though traditional Christians claim that enslavement to Christ is perfect freedom, non-Christians (that is, those without any conscious experience of Christ) have understandably had a hard time appreciating that claim.

Even if God sends no one to hell and grants universal salvation, even if man does not have to renounce his freedom to get to heaven, the Marxist would still rebel. The Marxist's attitude toward the universalist Christian would be analogous to the black militant's attitude toward the civil rights Negro. Black militants do not want to be *given* justice. They do not want to surrender their pride and dignity by accepting benevolence and charity. They want to *seize* justice and earn self-respect in the process. Only then will they really be free.

Human freedom is a central preoccupation for dialogical Christians and Marxists. Dialogical Marxists have attempted to meet the Christian's objection that Marxism enchains man to inexorable laws. They have sought to disavow the metaphysical and deterministic qualities that historical materialism seems to entail. Hence, they have gravitated toward the *young* Marx, whom they perceive to be an indeterminist. Simultaneously, dialogical Christians have attempted to meet the Marxist's objection that Christianity makes man the slave of a "great master." They have sought, with considerable difficulty, to dispel the notion that man is merely God's underling—without discarding the notion of a providential God.

To achieve this, Cox has promoted the idea that man is God's partner and co-worker.[52] Cox's God is, of course, always for man, never against him. He is not, in Will Herberg's words, "the biblical God who confronts sinful man as enemy before He comes out to meet repentant man as a Savior."[53] In fact, God is man's servant. In Cox's view, it was through Jesus that God showed his willingness "to become the *junior* partner in the asymmetric relationship [between man and God]."[54] A servant God of this sort can, of course, be used to service and justify any kind of human endeavor, from building a liberated society to primitive capitalist accumulation, from wars of national liberation to Americanization of the globe, from world government to world war. Cox uses this servant God in his dialogue with Marxism and enlists him in the realization of utopian and socialist objectives.

According to Cox, the task of the church is "to discern the action of God in the world and join in His work."[55] But how does one know what God is doing? How does one distinguish between volunteering in God's work and enlisting God in man's work? Curiously, these are not problems for Cox and most dialogical Christians. Their operational method may be summarized in the words of the old Unitarian maxim: "Whatever the unspoiled conscience of good men agree upon as fundamentally, ultimately, good is God Almighty's will." According to Cox's version of this maxim, God is "*whatever* it is within the vast spectacle of cosmic evolution which inspires and supports the endless struggle for liberation. . . ."[56] This is a way of saying that whatever Harvey Cox likes at a given moment is God. This is certainly a comforting notion; however, to the orthodox Christian, I suspect such a pliable God would be regarded as nothing but a manageable idol, a projection of human vanity.

If this servant God would not satisfy orthodox Christians, he would not satisfy Marxists either. It is clear that Cox's God, regardless of how immanent, in some sense does *act* in history. By definition the Coxian God always helps people, never constrains them. Even though this God is totally benign, the fact remains that he acts, and if he acts he limits human freedom and autonomy. From the viewpoint of the dialogical Marxist, we have not progressed very far from the tyrannical God of orthodoxy or the ontological metaphysics of historical materialism. Nevertheless, from a Marxist angle, the idea of a servant God is a dramatic improvement over traditional theology. Since God does not exist anyway, it is better to have one that reinforces human revolutionary ideals, rather than inhibits them. The philosophical concept of human autonomy may still be compromised, but from a practical point of view the task of enlisting Christians in Marxist causes is greatly facilitated. For example, Garaudy finds no difficulty in appropriating the Coxian motif for his own purposes: "if it is true that the God of the Bible becomes only manifest in history . . . can one not say that God is . . . wherever a new greatness is added to man—in scientific and technological discovery, in artistic creation and poetry, in the liberation of a people or a social revolution—wherever man becomes like unto the image of God . . . ?"[57] Garaudy, an atheist, finds no problem in affirming God's presence in human liberation. The reason seems to be that both Cox and Garaudy share a common idea of liberation (Garaudy's idea of liberation is discussed in Chapter 5). For Cox, salvation is not an eternal life beyond death, but the full liberation of mankind, by which he means a society where people no longer crave power and property, and no longer seek to manipulate other people.[58] It is apparent that Coxian liberation is nothing other than the non-alienating, classless society that dialogical and revisionist Marxists have been advocating. If Cox wants to attribute this society to the inspiration of an immanental God, why should the Marxist take umbrage? Maybe Cox feels inspired by some such God. That is his personal affair; the important thing is that he is working for, not against, liberation. The Marxist demand that Christians grant man full autonomy and full responsibility for creating a liberated world of the future has met with considerable success. What remains to be seen is how Christians are able to juggle the notion of a pliable, but manifest, Providence with the notion of authentic human freedom.

Some dialogical Christians perceive the contradiction between a God who acts and full human autonomy, and resolve it by opting for an immanent God (or Zeitgeist) who does not act at all. But others (like Moltmann and the early Cox) are so committed to a politician-God who acts that when they seek to heed the dialogical Marxist's demand for total human autonomy, they get trapped in their own rhetoric. The result is what could be called a *studied ambiguity*. On the one hand, they insist on an immanent God who, in some sense, acts as man's partner; but on the other hand, they insist that man is totally free and totally responsible for the future of the world. This is obviously contradictory. To invoke the concept of "dialectics" will do nothing to clarify the matter. Any action of God entails a limitation of human freedom. Otherwise, if man truly is free, all talk of God's "action" must be figurative (and deceptive). But if God does act, then man is not truly free. Divine action and human freedom are logically in a zero-sum relationship; the more divine action, the less human freedom, and vice versa.

Here I propose to explore Cox's development of this studied ambiguity over a ten-year period. I shall begin with his book, *God's Revolution and Man's Responsibility* (which is based on lectures delivered in 1963), and proceed to *The Secular City* (first edition, 1965; revised edition, 1966), his contributions to *The Secular City Debate* (1966), *On Not Leaving It to the Snake* (essays from 1964 to 1967), *The Feast of Fools* (1969), and *The Seduction of the Spirit* (1973). The first two books represent the "early" Cox, the next two represent his transitional period, and the last two represent the "later" Cox.

In *God's Revolution,* the emphasis is on man's response to God's initiative. Historical and political initiative lies in God's hands, not man's. God, with whom man may cooperate, is the author of change, from which man may benefit. "He [God] is renewing and recreating his world, and he wants us to be a part of his reconstructing activity."[59]

But Cox quickly shifts his ground and stresses human initiative. "Man is that creature who is created and called by God to shape and enact his own destiny. Whenever he relinquishes that privilege to someone else, he ceases to be a man."[60] This can only be understood to mean that man is fully man when he does not relinquish his destiny to external forces. However, Cox does not recognize the full force of his claim because the "someone else" he has in mind seems to be, not God, but such immanental powers as fate. "Fate is that over which man has no control. . . . But the Bible insists that God has made us free from fate. . . . God's program in history is to 'defatalize' human life, to put man's life into man's own hands and to give him the terrible responsibility of running it." Hence, it becomes clear that man is given his freedom from fate, his dominion over the world, and his responsibility for the future because "God makes us free. . . . He is pressing us into a situation in which we can no longer blame anyone else for what goes wrong including him. This is freedom."[61] The picture that emerges is one where God *compels* man to be free. In this role, God is active and responsible. But once man is free, God is no longer responsible for what man does with his freedom. Man's destiny is in his own hands and it is his "terrible responsibility." This is a kind of *procedural* freedom which God bestows upon man. God does not give man *substantive* freedoms such as freedom from war, injustice, and poverty. Rather, he forces man to be responsible for war, injustice, and poverty, and gives man the freedom to work out substantive solutions if he so chooses. God does not give man utopia; he merely gives man the freedom, hence the power, to achieve it if he is willing. The concept of human freedom offered here is intelligible, although it is compromised by the idea that procedural freedom is given to or forced upon man by an external force.

However, Cox's (limited) concept of freedom slips into unintelligibility when it becomes apparent that the freedom God bestows on man is substantive after all. Cox claims that God is breaking into history in the secular, peace, racial, scientific, and anticolonial revolutions. Not only that, but "our hope is . . . that God will make the world new, that God will reconstruct and reconstitute the world in the shape of his *shalom*." Cox defines *shalom* as "the exclusive content of the New Era. It is the character of the kingdom of God—the new regime of the Messiah. It is love, joy, and peace."[62] The logic here is clearly that man passively watches while God thrusts utopia upon him. This may be an attractive vision, but it certainly carries with it an anemic understanding of human *freedom*.

One's overall impression up to this point is that Cox is profoundly confused. This impression is not altered after examining *The Secular City*. Consider, for example, Cox's analysis of Communism: "For the orthodox Communist there is an inner logic in history which is not dependent on man, a meaning to which man must adjust his personal projects or suffer the consequences."[63] Cox calls this *fatalism*—that from which God has liberated man. He acknowledges that Communism is not a "vulgar" materialism which turns man into a robot. No, Communism allows for man's free will in rejecting the logic of history—but at man's own peril.

Cox denies, though, that his own views are fatalistic. However, it is interesting to note how his description of Communism is similar to his description of Hebrew prophecy, which he takes as his model for understanding history. Said Cox (elsewhere): "The prophets talk about the future in terms of what Yahweh will do [that is, punish his people] *unless his people change their ways.* Yahweh is free to change his mind. The future is *not* predetermined."[64] Cox interprets the main impact of prophecy as providing man with free responsibility for his future. But even if the future is not predetermined, it is clear that not man, but Yahweh (who sets the rules for the game, so to speak), is the truly free actor here. Cox actually grants man a very qualified kind of moral responsibility and a very conditional kind of freedom. What Cox is really saying is that people will find fulfillment if they conform to God's standards; if they do not, then disaster. This is structurally analogous to the Communist view that people will find fulfillment if they conform to the laws of history; if they do not, then they will perpetuate their bondage and perhaps bring self-destruction upon themselves. Both views can be seen as (benevolent) fatalisms and denials of human freedom.

Cox's treatment of human freedom is exceedingly vague and

succeeds merely in begging the question. He has said that "the elements of *divine initiative* and human response in the coming of the Kingdom are totally inseparable."[65] Note that the initiative here is still divine, not human. Human freedom is not even given the benefit of the doubt. Since God works in history, Cox continued, "the issue is whether history, and particularly revolution, is something that happens *to* man or something that man *does*. . . . Is man the subject or the object of social change?" Cox answered that he is both: "the secular city . . . stands for that point where social movement and *human initiative* intersect, where man is free not in spite of but because of the social matrix in which he lives."[66] But note that the initiative has subtly passed from God to man, and God is equated with the "social matrix" and the "social movement." Here God does not have initiative, but merely facilitates man's initiative.

One is tempted to pursue the identification of God with the social matrix or social movement. One might infer that Cox has some mechanism of social causation in mind, that his God is the Marxist "god" of History. But this inference is dashed when one comes upon Cox's insistence that "the future is not controlled by 'principalities and powers'—or their modern equivalents, economic and psychological determinants" and that "we are responsible for shaping the future."[67] One is left wondering what to make of Cox's allusion to God as the social matrix. Is Jesus, the "Son of God," to be understood as the "Son of the social matrix"?

There is some telltale evidence that Cox is not quite so sure about God's manifest action in history and the divine qualities of the social matrix, that Cox really has no idea whether historical initiative is God's or man's. In an article on the church in East Germany, he concluded by saying that "God is doing something in East Germany today. . . ."[68] But when he revised the essay for inclusion in a book of his essays, he altered the phrase to read: "*something important* is happening in East Germany today."[69] One gets the feeling that the word "God" functions in Cox's vocabulary as a metaphor for "something important," and as an instance of hyperbolic speech. Is God doing something, or is it just that something important is happening? This confusion is typical of theologians such as Cox who have no meaningful criterion for distinguishing between something that is happening in history because of God, and something that is just happening, period. One cannot avoid the conclusion that when a Christian confidently asserts that God is doing X, Y, and Z in profane history, what he *really* means to say is that X, Y, and Z conform to his political preconceptions of what is important—and desirable.

According to Cox, God cannot be spoken of metaphysically, but must be spoken of in a secular fashion. The way that is done is to talk of his political action in the secular world.[70] But clearly, any such talk presupposes a notion of divine initiative—a notion Cox has succeeded in reducing to unintelligibility. What are we to make of this God who is neither empirically verifiable, nor metaphysical, nor known through canonical revelation (as interpreted through the church)? Cox's God is so elusive and phantomlike, his discourse about God so blatantly "nonsensical" (as that term has been used by many analytic philosophers), that one must conclude that his God is nothing more than an emotive projection of whatever he happens to deem politically important—and desirable—at a given moment. (More orthodox God-talk may not be empirically verifiable either, but at least the outsider has an easier time discerning what is being talked about since such God-talk is rooted in a tradition of discourse that gives it a degree of coherence and predictability, a degree of intersubjectivity.) The only thing that saves Coxian God-talk from utter subjectivity and capriciousness is the way it dovetails with the imperatives of the Zeitgeist, hence giving it a certain coherence.

In his post-*Secular City* phases, Cox comes to deemphasize God's initiative and man's response, and to place exclusive emphasis on the unconditional autonomy of man and the unconditional openness of history. He still believes in the possibility of speaking in a secular (or political) fashion about God; however, he has warned that such speech about God "has theological dimensions far more baffling than those indicated in *The Secular City*." (One wonders how much more bafflement one can stand!) He claims that his critics have turned him "toward the future, where if man meets God again, that encounter must take place."[71] Cox comes to talk of the God of the future who is located, not above history, but ahead of history, and who anchors or guarantees the openness of history and human freedom. Although God is responsible for the openness of the future, man is responsible for the content of that future. Indeed, because God keeps man's future undetermined, man really has no choice but to take responsibility for it. Here the influence of both Moltmann and Leslie Dewart on the development of Cox's thought is evident.[72]

But between Moltmann and Dewart only Dewart is able to avoid falling into studied ambiguity on the question of human freedom, and on this question the later Cox follows Dewart's lead more than Moltmann's. Dewart simply rejects the idea that God acts. His God is impersonal and does not "exist" as a being or as Being itself; rather God is "presence" (not *a* "presence," simply "presence"). In some sense it is this presence that guarantees human freedom and history's openness. Whether, or how, this is the case, this God clearly poses no obstacle to human freedom.[73] Cox was so impressed with Dewart that he said: "we either move along the road Dewart has staked out or else we abandon any pretense that we can find a viable doctrine of God for our time."[74]

Cox argues along with Dewart that the belief in God's omnipotence must be transformed into a belief in the radical openness of history. He correctly perceives that this would meet a major Marxist criticism of Christianity, namely, that Christianity does not allow man to take full control of his future. But Cox also correctly perceives that Marxism itself is rather fuzzy on this point. There is a very strong suggestion in Marxism that there is an inner logic to history to which man must conform in order to be free. From this Cox concludes that Christianity must give man more freedom to determine his future than Marxism does, that Christianity "must break its ties with any belief in a fixed plan being worked out in history," and must understand God as "that unconditionally open future which elicits man's unreserved freedom in shaping his own future."[75]

Cox tends to look at the future not as a mere extrapolation of the present, not as something already contained in the seeds of the present, but as open to radically new possibilities. He strongly rejects any teleology because it "obscures the fact that history is radically open, has no predetermined end, and will go only where man takes it and nowhere else."[76]

By this point, Cox's studied ambiguity has dissolved. He has clearly opted for human freedom; however, his notion of God is perhaps more slippery, more "baffling," than ever. Said William Hamilton, a self-proclaimed Christian-atheist: "when Harvey Cox names 'openness to the future' as God, I want to say, 'Yes one ought to be open to the future,' but I see no grounds for naming this God."[77] It certainly remains unclear what an open future has to do with God.

Yet it is quite clear that with this radical emphasis on an open future, both Gnostic and Pelagian themes come into play. World denial is a perennial Gnostic theme, whether it be the rejection of this world *(kosmos)* "below" as in ancient Gnosticism or of this world *(kosmos)* "behind" as in the case of modern Gnosticism. In the latter case it is the Spirit of the World which is the carrier of the promise of a new world in the future.

On the other hand, the exaltation of man's freedom and sovereign ability to make moral and responsible choices and work out his own salvation, and the relegation of God and his grace to a passive role is a perennial Pelagian theme. Whereas the Gnostics demonized the sovereign and providential God of creation and turned to a "God above God," Cox eviscerates him by subordinating him to the Zeitgeist.

Much of the Marxist-Christian dialogue is taken up with Marxists and Christians seeking to surpass one another in their declarations of fealty to human freedom and self-determination. Cox clearly speaks for this preoccupation, even going so far as to claim epistemological status for the concept of human freedom: "Jesus said that if we know the truth it will make us free. We must now also recognize that whatever makes us free is *truth*."[78] Ironically, absolute freedom is characteristically an existentialist concern, not a Marxist or Christian concern. It is strange that Marxists and Christians should find common ground on the alien turf of existentialism. Even more bizarre is how, in order to affirm human freedom, Marxists and Christians must sacrifice the *basis* for their hope, that is, historical materialism and divine Providence, respectively.

In espousing unequivocal human freedom, then, Cox has clearly lost even his residual faith in God. All he has left is a faith in hope, which is a vacuous and baseless hope. He has admitted as much himself: "Ours is a more or less formless hope, but a hope nonetheless. It is a hope in search of content, a hope that some form of hope will once again be made available to us."[79] Elsewhere, Cox added: "What we have today is a hope without a persuasive dogmatic base or clear empirical confirmation or even specific content. We hope even when we cannot name the source. We hope, among other things, that hope itself will not disappear. If challenged to say whether there is any real ground for such a faith, we can only say, 'We hope so.' "[80] Cox, who claims to have a theology of hope, really has come up with a theology of freedom.

It is curious that he should place so much emphasis on his hope for the eschatological future when he can offer no reason for having any such hope. To damn his politicotheological philosophy as sheer fantasy seems appropriate. But Cox is willing to take that criticism—and turn it to his own advantage, so he thinks. In *The Feast of Fools,* he admits that hope and fantasy are directly related. He calls for a theology of political fantasy, a utopian politics. He urges religion to contribute to society's capacity for self-transcendence: "It does so by symbolizing an ideal toward which to strive, and by doing so with enough *emotional magnetism* to provide a powerful source of *motivation.*"[81] It is Cox's conviction that religion is not only an opiate but also a cry of the oppressed, a protest, and a potent stimulus for insurrection (a conviction increasingly shared by dialogical Marxists). When he says that the truth of religion is its capacity to facilitate human liberation, he does not mean "truth" in its cognitive sense. Rather, religion manifests a pragmatic or instrumental truth, an emotive or noncognitive truth. Its truth is really its ability to motivate: "A 'religious symbol' is defined not by its *content* but by its *relative degree of cultural power.*"[82] Such religious truth is found in all religions; however, the various and mutually exclusive doctrines of all these religions present no problem so far as "truth" is concerned: "We don't ask . . . how *much* to believe, or *whether* to believe this or that. Rather we are looking for, and finding occasionally, a *way* to embrace it all. Not all, really, but all that can contribute to our inner and outer liberation."[83]

Cox wants to unmask the way religious myths have repressed people and then proceed to reconstruct these myths so they can be used to incite credulous people to radical and insurrectionary action. Cox unconsciously sets himself up as an elitist myth-manipulator much as Georges Sorel did early in this century with his "myth of the General Strike." It goes without saying that orthodox Christians (or Moslems, et al.) would likely be insulted by this attempt to use their beliefs as mere tools to mobilize people for political ends. Nevertheless, this is an interesting solution to the search by New Left intellectuals for a lever of social change in the wake of their disillusionment with the standard Marxist lever, the proletariat.

In the meantime, however, Cox lapses back into his studied ambiguity on the question of human autonomy. In *The Seduction of the Spirit,* he continues his theology of fantasy and hope; however, he drops his emphasis on unfettered human freedom and an inactive God, and subordinates freedom to his concept of liberation. Liberation does not mean the freedom to create or not create the New Jerusalem; it *is* the New Jerusalem. It is "paradoxically . . . both a task and a gift. It will be a city they [men and women] build and also simply receive, a result combining the keenest human dexterity with that unpredictable input from elsewhere that still merits the term 'grace.' "[84] But Cox does not really mean the grace of God. He turns around and subordinates this "grace" to human freedom. There is evidence that "grace" is really a procedural freedom granted man by God, much like Christ's Resurrection is supposed to have marked the liberation of man from the bonds of Original Sin. What man does with his freedom, whether he builds the New Jerusalem or not, ultimately depends on man: "Man's only destiny is to use his *God-given freedom* to shape and achieve his destiny for himself. If he refuses this destiny, then nothing can save him . . . nothing at all."[85] Indeed, salvation is not guaranteed, either by grace or human freedom; destruction is an open possibility. Salvation is neither otherworldly nor individualistic; either everyone is saved in this world or no one is. As Cox said elsewhere: "If man is saved or damned . . . he is so in inextrica-

ble solidarity with the whole human family."[86] The symbolism
here is Manichean, not Christian. According to Manicheanism
(a variant of Gnosticism), God and Satan, Light and Darkness,
are two eternal and equally powerful forces. In theory at least, it
is as conceivable for Darkness to vanquish Light in the end as
vice versa. Wherever Cox conceives of human freedom as ultimate and unqualified (whether a gift or not), this Manichean
logic is unavoidable. We shall meet this implied Manicheanism
again in Moltmann.

Whether Cox flounders in a studied ambiguity or makes a
clear decision in favor of human autonomy, the self-salvific imperative of building the Kingdom of God on earth by human
effort remains constant. Depsite some vivid messianic prose
and occasional outbursts of enthusiasm for revolution (especially in Latin America), he continues to repudiate the idea of a
terminal point in history (as well as a life beyond death): "the
Messiah is always the one who *will* come. . . . There is no 'final
solution' for anything."[87]

His point of view remains consistently antisupernaturalist. Although he does talk about transcendence, it is always a thisworldly transcendence: "our search for God is directed toward
the transcendence that is present in *this* world, not in some
other."[88] Hence, despite his recent affection for the accoutre-
ments of religion, both Christian and non-Christian (an affection faithfully in tune with the latest cultural trends), Cox remains a consistent secularist, albeit a secularist with a difference. As long as he presses for the earthly New Jerusalem, his
thought contains the seeds of sacralism and theocracy. When
he compresses the difference between the sacred and the secular, it appears as if he is dismissing the sacred. However, he
seeks to infuse the secular world (the only world there is) with
a sacred quality (via the metaphor of the Kingdom of God). We
have once again the Gnostic urge to redivinize the world.

This resacralization tendency is apparent in the early Cox where God is active in secular history. Here Cox says that God must be spoken of as a political issue; he confidently points to the activity of the politician-God and implores man to join in his work. But if God is a political issue, sin is likewise. Since God helps to usher in the secular city, indifference or resistance to that City of Man constitutes sin.[89] The inevitable (though unintended) effect is to advance a black-versus-white Manichean political ethos. When a certain political action, event, or process is deemed of God, and obstruction is construed as sin, there would seem to be little room left for honest disagreement. When people with this mentality achieve political power the temptation to theocracy would seem to be intense.

This implicit approval of theocracy is contrary to Cox's intention in that he disavows any "final solution" and has consistently employed anticlerical and antisacral rhetoric. But the logic of his position leads precisely to the investing of political leaders and movements with sacred, hence absolute, significance. This would especially be the case where the leader of a movement is charismatic, "prophetic," and has a special "gift" for discerning the Zeitgeist or God's hand in the world of politics. This is indeed the classical formula for totalitarian movements. (Even though the God of the later Cox is usually inactive, the effect is roughly the same since the sacred Kingdom of God is ever impinging upon the politics of the present from the future. For details on this, see the section on Moltmann.)

This compulsion toward theocracy is characteristic of the frequently mingled traditions of enthusiasm (see page 61) and heretical chiliasm. "Always the enthusiast hankers after a theocracy . . . ," Ronald Knox has said.[90] Joachim's Third Age was pure theocracy. Roland H. Bainton has called Muentzer the "progenitor of the Protestant theocratic idea."[91] The heretical chiliasts were, to a man, adamant foes of the Constantinian church of Christendom. But instead of dismantling Constantinianism by driving a wedge between the sacred and the secular, religion and politics, they practiced a Constantinianism with a vengeance. This ironic stance is typical of Cox and dialogical Christians in general. On the one hand, they condemn the existing church for its vestigial clericalism. But instead of seeking to grant full autonomy to the temporal order, they proceed to sacralize it with militant zeal. This tendency has provoked Paul Ramsey to point to the "oddity" whereby the social ethics of contemporary "secular" Christian activists "evidences less acknowledgment of the separation between the church and the office of magistrate or citizen than was clearly acknowledged by the great cultural churches of the past. . . ."[92]

JUERGEN MOLTMANN

Juergen Moltmann is regarded by many observers of the world's leading theologians as the most outstanding living Protestant theologian. In 1974, the editors of seven church periodicals in the United States and Canada cited Moltmann as one of the major shapers of current Christian thought and life, "the most dominant theological presence of our time." Moltmann was recognized as this generation's leading contender to stand alongside the theological giants of the previous generation (such as Karl Barth, Paul Tillich, Emil Brunner, Rudolf Bultmann, Reinhold Niebuhr, and Dietrich Bonhoeffer). Furthermore, he was commended for having opened "the theological door for the Latin American priests and laity [such as Rubém Alves and Gustavo Gutiérrez] who mix Christian and Marxist ideologies."[93]

Moltmann is a Professor of Systematic Theology at the University of Tuebingen. He has been sympathetic to the German New Left and student movement, and critical of the German university system and positivistic epistemologies.

Of all the "new" theologies born in the 1960s, Moltmann's theology of hope is the one most likely to last, and the only one that shows signs of developing into a genuinely systematic theology.

Moltmann comes out of the Protestant Reformed tradition although his denominational background does not bear heavily on his thinking. As a matter of fact, like Cox, he identifies more with the heretical chiliasts and the Radical Reformation than with Calvin and the Magisterial Reformation. It is through the heretical chiliasts that Moltmann feels he can best make contact with Marxists (in particular, Ernst Bloch, to whom much of his early work is a response). He recognizes the affinity between the heretical chiliasts and modern socialism: "Since the time of Joachim di Fiore in the Middle Ages, hope in the 'new age' . . . has influenced all revolutionary movements from the Renaissance through the Reformation to the English, French, and Russian revolutions." In fact, his respect for heresy goes all the way back to the ancient Church: "When the universal church excluded Marcion [the Gnostic] as a heretic, it lost for itself the category of the new. As is always the case with the exclusion of heresies, the church became more united, but also poorer."[94]

Like Cox, Moltmann embodies the three basic heresies we have been discussing: (1) He affirms the potential perfectibility of creation: "The creation is . . . an open creation. It is open for its own destruction as well as its redemption in a new creation. It is not perfect but perfectible."[95] His understanding of human nature undermines the doctrine of Original Sin. He understands human nature in terms of man's natural possibilities for future perfection. Hence, human nature is not fixed: "Mankind does not have a single, universal nature. . . . To the depths of his 'innermost being,' man is ambiguous, changeable and open."[96] As mentioned above (on page 36), he sees Original Sin more in terms of docility than Promethean hubris.

Because man's nature is not immutable, (2) man's building of the Kingdom of God on earth becomes a live possibility. In fact, the future is an open process, so open that "the salvation and destruction, the righteousness and annihilation of the world are at stake."[97] Yet, Moltmann does see that God has a role to play in this process. However, he has difficulty fitting the *Christian* God into his design. For if the world could end in destruction, Moltmann's God would have been powerless to prevent it and guarantee a happy future for the Kingdom. Either all talk about God would seem to be rhetorical or we have the makings of a Manichean cosmology. On the other hand, if Moltmann's God is not powerless to prevent destruction but simply does not desire to prevent it, then we have the Gnostic creator-God who is undoubtedly evil.

To be sure, orthodoxy allows for the possibility that the world will end in destruction; however, it will be executed by God, not by something that will happen outside his power and will. Furthermore, if God were to destroy the world (a belief orthodoxy does not seem to require), it would be a prelude to the final triumph of good over evil—the Kingdom of God, heaven and hell. However, Moltmann will have nothing to do with the traditional Christian heaven, which he regards as "old and repressive." He contends that Christianity "dare not dream away any longer about an eternity beyond time. It must bring the hoped-for future into practical contact with the misery of the present."[98]

Moltmann is unwilling to wait upon God for the eschatological transformation: "The coming lordship of the risen Christ cannot be merely hoped for and awaited."[99] He calls upon man to transform the face of the world through political activism.

Moltmann holds (3) a skeptical view of biblical authority and makes what appears to be a self-consciously Hegelian identification of God with the Spirit of the Age as it works itself out in the secular world. He unambiguously asserts a concept of ongoing or "progressive" revelation which means that "the impulse of the Christian spirit in the history of the West links up again and again with the *spirit of the modern age* and produces progressively better views of the world and of life." It also means that "the progress of the human spirit can be interpreted as the self-movement of absolute Spirit."[100]

God is identified with the Spirit of the Age and with its concrete manifestations, namely, political revolutions. Moltmann claims that the petrification of human societies provokes the Spirit to revolution. He asks himself "whether one can attribute historical processes of this kind to the Holy Spirit." His answer is: "I think one can do this."[101] He further suggests that when the hope for the Kingdom is joined with Herbert Marcuse's social analysis, the hope for the Kingdom can become practical and real.[102]

Moltmann speculates that the atheist may be closer to God than the religious person,[103] and he tends to see the Holy Spirit as absent from the church while present to the world through the Zeitgeist. He is inclined to see the church as apostate and the "spirit of the modern age" as truly Christian. Like Cox, he argues that secularization was no apostasy, but rather a way in which eschatological hopes "have emigrated from the church and have been invested in revolutions and rapid social change." He calls on the church to experience a rebirth to overcome this "schism."[104] The church is identified with apostasy and is urged to conform and convert to the truth embodied in the world and its spirit. This inversion of traditional categories is akin to Cox's inclination to view orthodox Christians as the real heretics.

Moltmann is unable to give a satisfactory response to the question of whether man is an autonomous or heteronomous being. Although he tries hard to affirm human freedom in an open future, his need to retain his theistic credentials forces him to affirm that the future of man *is* God, that the God of the future exerts a "pull" on man in the present, that the Kingdom is not built only by man, and that the Holy Spirit infuses the Spirit of the Age. This straddling of the fence puts Moltmann in a position of studied ambiguity not unlike that of the early Cox. However, unlike Cox, he does not tend to resolve the contradiction by opting for one of the horns of the dilemma.

Moltmann's God is in the future; in a strict sense, he cannot be said to exist. Hence, man is free. Furthermore, God is not only man's future, he is in some way the guarantor of an open and undetermined future where man has the responsibility for constructing the Kingdom. For example, Moltmann has argued that man "cannot passively wait for this future. . . . Rather, he must seek this future, strive for it, and . . . realize it already here according to the measure of possibilities." He explicitly calls for a "political theology," meaning that theology becomes relevant through politics.[105] However, he obscures his point by saying that "it is unreal to anticipate and work for this future if this future does not come toward us. The future in which we hope is never identical with the successes of our activity. . . ."[106] The future (God) impinges on the present so that God can be pictured, not as above man, but as ahead of man, leading him forward (through the agency of the Zeitgeist). But inasmuch as the future determines the present, it is difficult to understand how man can be said to be free and the future open. A principle of determinism is still operative. Hence, the open future would seem not to be open, but full of predetermined content.

Elsewhere Moltmann says that the future is open because it has nothing to do with destiny or fatalism.[107] Yet, he can proceed to claim that the realization of the hoped-for future "is in God's hands. The hoped-for future . . . is God's future. . . . [which] exerts an influence in the present. . . ."[108] He asserts that since the future lies in God's hands it cannot lie in the hands of "blind fate." However, to the non-Christian, especially the Marxist, this fine distinction between God and fate (also found in Cox) must be unsatisfactory. Both God (however benign) and fate (however blind) deny people their freedom and self-determination.

Yet, Moltmann wants to say that without God man could not be free: "God reveals his future to men and has, thereby, *granted* them freedom." Hence, "The prospect of this future coming from God already opens up here and now an open space of change and freedom which must be shaped with responsibility and confidence."[109] Again, as with the early Cox, we see the word "freedom" being used in a highly qualified way; man is *given* his freedom to work with God (but certainly not against God).

Also like Cox, Moltmann wants to say that man is God's co-worker in the building of the Kingdom. Christian hope must be militant because the Kingdom does not "simply lie in readiness." Hence, Christians "must enter the battle for God's righteousness on earth politically in the battle against human misery." In this context he raises the theodicy problem: "The question: if God is, why is there still evil in the world? becomes an accusation not against God, but against ourselves. . . ."[110] But in wiping away the theodicy problem he wipes away his own concept of human partnership with God in building the Kingdom; God is exonerated of responsibility for evil because he plays no role in expunging it—that is the human task. But Moltmann immediately shifts his ground again: "The real future is not identical with the successes of our activity. It must come towards us in order that our activity be 'not in vain' (1 Cor. 15, 58)."[111] If this is so, then the theodicy question comes right back and humans again have a motive for accusing God of responsibility for evil (for example, "Why doesn't God 'come towards us' faster?") as well as a motive for unmilitant resignation. (Curiously, in a subsequent book, Moltmann gave up on the theodicy question, saying that it "does not permit an explanation."[112])

When Moltmann moves in the direction of a future full of predetermined content he shows that his concern is for human success, not human freedom: "In order to be able to act with certainty . . . we need the consciousness that this future is not built with our own hands but comes towards us. . . ."[113] The assurance that the future is coming toward us would seem to make waiting as attractive an option as acting. Furthermore, how can an *assured* future be an *open* future? Here human freedom must be a coerced freedom. (The basis for Moltmann's assurance is discussed below.)

Indeed, Moltmann has said that people acquire freedom by participating in the creative freedom of God: "One acquires social, political, and world-surpassing freedom from God, not against him."[114] But this is at best a vicarious freedom. It is not much different from Engels's formula (almost universally derogated by dialogical Marxists and dialogical Christians) that freedom is the recognition of historical necessity, that freedom is gained from history, not against it. Of course, it was just this kind of understanding of freedom that provided justification for the Stalinist dictatorship's practice of forcing the masses to be "free." It is highly interesting that Moltmann has defended the anti-Stalinist and libertarian socialism of Adam Schaff and Leszek Kolakowski in such terms as these: "It is impossible to make people happy by force."[115] But is it any more possible to make people free by force? Is it possible to absorb man into the creative freedom of the Godhead and still talk about human freedom? These are the kinds of questions a dialogical Marxist would certainly want to ask.

Moltmann holds that there is no final consummation to the Kingdom within history. He flatly states that "there can be no chiliastic perfection . . . in history."[116] He tells Marxists not to feel secure in their earthly hope because *this* earth will pass away: "There is salvation only in the new creation of heaven and earth. . . ." He criticizes Bloch for having no hope to offer the dead, retorting that God "will raise the dead."[117] And yet he has ridiculed the idea of an "eternity beyond time" (see p. 92 above).

His God is not a miracle-working supernatural being. Moltmann identifies with a theology that "has been emancipated from all metaphysics." Nevertheless, he insists that there will be a resurrection of the dead and that there is a wider horizon than history, "an eschaton of all history which is itself historical and yet no longer historical"[118]—all of which sounds suspiciously metaphysical. Moltmann seems unable to make up his mind. The clarity and effectiveness of his system falters on an eschatological equivocation. By introducing the idea of personal survival beyond death (however vague he is about it), he risks compromising the urgency of his political theology. He wants to motivate people to take decisive action to better the world; he wants them to know they are free to act. And yet, almost like an insurance policy, he wants a God safely ensconced in a future somewhere bordering a "beyond history," perhaps in case things do not work out. Hence, the clarity of his appeal is subverted by his reintroduction of seemingly metaphysical and otherworldly thoughts which stand in stark contrast to his calls for people to act and take responsibility for an open future. Hope for a life beyond death may not dampen Moltmann's own enthusiasm for changing the world; however, history tells us that it has had that effect on others in the past, and common sense tells us that it will have that effect on others in the future.

Moltmann speaks of the "doubleness of . . . redemption and mobilization."[119] Often one gets the impression that Moltmann's Kingdom, just as Cox's Kingdom, functions as a

Sorelian mobilizing myth, as when he said: "The expectation of the promised future of the kingdom of God which is coming to man . . . makes us ready to expend ourselves unrestrainedly and unreservedly. . . ."[120] This human expense is necessary because of Moltmann's commitment that the coming of the Kingdom requires human action, human risk.[121] If it turns out that Moltmann is really serious about the openness of the future, then his eschatology can easily be seen to be an energizing myth. Walter H. Capps has observed that hope theology is not a demythologizing movement, but a remythologizing one: "the task is to find the story which is disclosive, the image which is inciteful. . . ."[122] We see in Moltmann, as in Cox, an exploitative and noncognitive approach to Christian doctrines and a tendency toward elitist myth-manipulation. How ironic it would be if the widely celebrated theology of hope is nothing but a New Left version of the power of positive thinking! Whatever the case, Moltmann has failed to integrate full human freedom and initiative with a real God who is more than a myth.

It is worth taking a closer look at Moltmann's doctrine of God. His God is "a God with 'future as his essential nature' . . . whom we therefore cannot really have in us or over us. . . ."[123] Quite literally, God does *not exist,* although he will in the future. God is not a supernatural, eternal, absolute being who is found beyond or behind history and the world. Yet, God will be found, will exist, in the future of the world and man (which is as yet nonexistent). With God safely tucked away in the future, human beings are free to create their future.

And yet, as Rosemary Ruether has said, there is an "apparent assumption that this future has power because it will finally come."[124] Since the future is always drawing the present unto itself, God influences the present. But when God is invested with the power to act on the present, man's freedom to do as he chooses is proportionately diminished. In essence, this God "ahead" of man acts very much like the God "above" man. It is difficult to see what is gained in terms of human freedom by placing God in the future if he still impinges on the here and now.

The notion that the future determines the present is baffling because it reverses our conventional understanding of causality where the past determines the present and the present determines the future. Nevertheless, it is clear (though perhaps not to Moltmann) that we are still employing a deterministic outlook.

Moltmann's motive for placing God in the future is to sidestep the old debate between theists and atheists as to whether God exists, and to safeguard both God's reality and man's freedom. Said Moltmann: "In the debate between theism, which says 'God is,' and atheism, which claims 'God is not,' eschatological theology . . . can say: God's being is coming. . . ."[125] It is astonishing that Moltmann thinks this solves anything. There is nothing in this position which compels the atheist to concede that, yes, God will exist in the future; for, as Langdon Gilkey has said, "the God who 'will be' is *also* balanced by the God who 'will not be.' "[126]

One wonders how serious Moltmann is about a God who exists in the future and has an impact on the present—when the future does not even exist! How literally does the future determine the present? Moltmann's doctrine of God would seem to trade on deliberate bafflement, hence provoking one to ask if it is not all "an evasion, an elusive way of keeping theology going without saying much of anything at all?"[127]

One of Moltmann's most nettlesome problems is epistemological. If God does not now exist, we cannot know anything about him from the present or the past. The Bible cannot be understood as inspired by God because God does not yet exist.

Hence, the Bible can tell us nothing authoritative about God or his alleged promises. If God is exclusively future, as Moltmann insists, there is no way of knowing *anything* about him (not even that he is exclusively future) and there is no point in pretending that the Bible can shed any light on the subject. Nevertheless, Moltmann is apparently uncomfortable with these implications of his position, for he persists (inexplicably) in granting a modicum of epistemological significance to the Bible.

As might be expected, Moltmann's treatment of the Bible is unusual. Although he is generally skeptical of the biblical record, he insists on the physical Resurrection of Christ; however, he understands it only "in the *modus* of promise. It has its time still ahead of it, is grasped as a 'historic phenomenon' only in its relation to *its* future. . . ."[128] Obviously, Moltmann cannot simply assert that God did in fact raise Christ from the dead since God did not then exist. What Moltmann is saying is that we *know* something to be true in the past because it will be shown to be true in the future. This is circular reasoning, for how do we know it *will* be shown to be true?

For Moltmann, the truth of the Bible will be made known in the future, and since man is given an activist role in shaping the future, man himself in a sense validates the Bible. Of the Bible, Moltmann said: "It provides no final revelation, but. . . . is valid to the extent it is *made* valid."[129] But what if one preferred the Koran to the Bible? Can the truth of the Koran (or any other sacred or special book) be validated in the future by simply making it valid? If so, one would have to know in advance why the Bible is to be preferred to any other book—something Moltmann neglects to do. Indeed, as Cox has shown, if the search for inciteful myths is central, there is no reason not to be eclectic, not to investigate non-Christian religions.

But Moltmann also speaks of the future as something that comes toward us, as if it were possessed of predetermined content. But in this case one wonders how we can know the future will have anything to do with the Bible, and why the future will prove the truth of the Bible instead of the truth of the Koran.

Since Moltmann is offering us a theology of hope, he is obliged to indicate what the basis of his hope is. For the Christian, "Faith gives substance to our hopes . . ." (Hebrews 11:1 NEB). However, Moltmann's hope, like Cox's, has no substantive basis in the Christian faith; instead, it rests on the selection of volatile myths. One problem here is that it is impossible to *decide* to believe in myths, that is, to believe in something one does not actually believe in. As Alasdair MacIntyre put it: "Suppose that you ask me whether I believe it is going to rain tomorrow, and I reply that I do not know. Suppose that you then urge me to choose to believe it is going to rain tomorrow. I will be unable to do so, not because of any failure of effort but simply because anything that is summoned up by an act of will does not qualify as a belief—although it may qualify as a hope or wish."[130]

The ultimate appeal of Moltmann's hope is that God can be trusted to create a new heaven and a new earth (the Kingdom of God) because he raised Jesus from the dead.[131] But since Moltmann can offer no reason (right now) for believing in the Resurrection, there does not appear to be any reason to hope.

In sum, Moltmann (much like Cox) has no basis for his hope. It goes without saying that he has no empirical basis. But he even has no basis in the Christian faith. Conformity with internal language norms (the Scriptures and tradition) governs what is warranted Christian speech. Since Moltmann does not adhere to those norms, his hope has no basis beyond his private speculations and desires. Curiously, he himself would seem to have been aware of this when he said the following about the quality of his certainty: "we can find certainty only in complete uncertainty."[132] If one subscribes to the normal canons of logic, this admission must be recognized as an act of intellectual suicide.

Not surprisingly, Moltmann has characterized his hope as "a 'passion for the impossible,' the not yet possible." Hence, he has denounced the "historical-positivistic fetishism of facts."[133] The world cannot be understood as "a rigid cosmos of established facts and eternal laws. For where there is no longer any possibility of anything new happening, there hope also comes to an end and loses all prospect of the realizing of what it hopes for. Only when the world itself is 'full of all kinds of possibilities' can hope become effective in love."[134] So, instead of searching the world for evidence of his utopian hope (as Marx did), he cavalierly redefines the nature of reality to accommodate his wishes. But he does not realize that by so defining reality he destroys the uniqueness of Christ's Resurrection; in a world where there are all kinds of possibilities and the power of mere facts has been transcended, there is nothing necessarily miraculous about the raising of Christ from the dead, or the ascension of Mohammed, or any other "unscientific" claim or magical event. It would even be possible to manufacture unicorns or a deity, or perhaps a hydra-headed monster or a devil with horns and red hair. Moltmann is seemingly unhappy with the Christian dedivinization of the pagan world laden with gods. As with Cox, what we have is that Gnostic urge to redivinize the world.

Basically, Moltmann's position is that God resides in the future whereas the past is godforsaken. The present is where the future impinges on the past; since God never becomes a part of any present, man remains free. Thus, the ongoing present continues to be godforsaken. What Moltmann is offering us is a radically dualistic picture of the world, a temporal (not spatial) dualism. For example, he has said that the great battle for

Christ's freedom is being fought today between the past, which he identifies with "sin, law and death," and the future, which he identifies with "spirit, justice and freedom."[135] He urges Christians to "love the future appearance of Christ" and to take "flight from the world."[136] All this smacks of modern Gnostic world-denial. Actually Moltmann seems to be somewhat aware of his affinity with the Gnostic tradition. Said he: "In Marxism the ideas of self-alienation and total reappropriation of true human essence are . . . of Gnostic origin. At one time Christianity absorbed the radical transcendence of Gnostic freedom, and can do so again today, if this freedom is not understood to be world-fleeing and otherworldly, but future-desiring, critical, and thisworldly, that is, historical. For the Christian God is not the 'Totally Other' of [ancient] Gnosticism but the 'Total Revolutionary'."[137] This future-dimensional, "Total Revolutionary" God is, as I have argued, the god of modern Gnosticism.

Furthermore, if God resides only in the future, not only is it impossible to make sense of divine revelation and such doctrines as the Incarnation and the Resurrection, but the doctrine of Creation also becomes meaningless. The creator of this world could not possibly be the God in whom Moltmann hopes. One would be led to believe that the creator-God is an evil God as Marcion and the Gnostics contended. If indeed the creator-God is evil, then the theodicy problem, which gave Moltmann so much trouble and which is at the root of the Gnostic passion, would be resolved.[138] Curiously, the God of the Gnostics was so elusive and remote, so far beyond ordinary human conceptions that, like Moltmann, they even referred to their God as the "non-being God."[139] Could this be one reason why Moltmann has shown sympathy for Marcion in particular (see page 91) and the Gnostic tradition in general?

Also, since in the present man is free, free to construct the

Kingdom, he is also free from grace. This of course is the classic Pelagian heresy whereby man is possessed of such freedom that Original Sin has no power over him and he is able to do good outside of God's grace. Furthermore, when the eschatological future finally does arrive and God will be fully God, all talk of freedom and secularity will be obsolete. As with Cox, we will have a sacralized society, a theocracy, wherein disagreement is tantamount to sin.[140]

Moltmann is sometimes interpreted as offering a *processive* view of God. He is thought to mean that since God will become fully God in the eschatological future, in the meantime God grows and matures as humanity and the world grow and mature. Moltmann has given credence to this interpretation with these words: "God cannot only be thought of as the future of the contemporary present, but must also be understood as the future of past presence."[141] In a sense, then, God can be understood to have left his mark on the past. Therefore, the past is not entirely godforsaken. But since God will only be fully God in the future, God must grow with the process of time. No other option seems to satisfy both the Moltmannian proposition that "God will be" and the Moltmannian intimation that "God was." If the God that will be has already touched past events, then either (1) we have a God who grows, or (2) Moltmann is not really serious about a God as "the future of past presence," or (3) we have the standard Christian notion of God as past, present, and future (which is the least likely of these options because it would destroy the originality of much of Moltmann's thought).

We may not have a sovereign creator-God in the processive view, but we do have a God who cannot be restricted to a future dimension, a God who leaves traces of his deeds and grace in his path. Unfortunately, this *becoming* God has not impressed dialogical Marxists. According to Bloch, "the world is not a machine for manufacturing such a supreme person, such a 'gaseous vertebrate' (as Haeckel rightly called it)."[142] Garaudy registered his objection in these terms: "it is impossible to conceive of a God who is always in process of making himself, in process of being born."[143]

The problem here is that such a processive view loses the sense of the radically *new* breaking into history from the future on which Moltmann insists. Process thought tends to view the future as an extrapolation from what is already present and sacrifices the idea that the future is really open to all sorts of radical possibilities. Furthermore, the processive view is at odds with Moltmann's basic insight that God does not grow out of the past but comes at us. Moltmann's God is the *coming* God, not the *becoming* God. I suspect that Moltmann is not really serious about a God as "the future of past presence."

In conclusion, not only does Moltmann's Christianity, which seeks to conform to Marxist aspirations, take significant leave of normative Christianity, it is also riddled with obscurity and conceptual confusion. Of course, Harvey Cox has fared no better.

Nevertheless, Moltmann does seem more conscious of the ephemeral and conditioned character of dialogical Christianity than does Cox. In 1972, Moltmann confessed that his hope theology was a product of the optimistic sensibility of the 1960s, in particular "the enthusiasm of the Kennedy era, the new 'socialism with a human face' in Czechoslovakia, the 'revolution of rising expectations' in the third world, Vatican II in the Roman Catholic Church, and the socio-political upsurge in the ecumenical movement."[144] Now that the optimistic mood has waned (temporarily), the theology of hope seems curiously sterile. Moltmann is now willing to admit that his hope theology will have to be revised so as to come to grips better with tragedy, frustration, evil, and death. Perhaps Moltmann is now better able to see the peril of building his thought on the shifting sands of cultural sensibility, to see that if one has any regard for truth, one will turn away from fickle cultural moods. But there is a larger issue here, of which Moltmann is only dimly aware as yet. It is perilous to claim validation for one's theology on the grounds that it has been tailored to fit the Spirit of the Age, especially since the heritage and original inspiration of Christianity are so fundamentally alien to that Spirit.

With the publication of *Der gekreuzigte Gott (The Crucified God)* in 1972, Moltmann clearly took a major step in the development of his thought—a step he had been hinting at in other writings. He seems vaguely aware that Christians lose their raison d'être when they chase after the Zeitgeist: "Does not theology lose its Christian identity if it is still determined to do nothing more than to adapt itself to the constantly changing 'spirit of the time'?"[145] Moltmann is now more aware that evil, suffering, and disappointment are part of the human condition, and that Christianity has something unique to say about these phenomena, and hence that to lose one's Christian identity is to lose something of value.

Moltmann believes that to make sense of human suffering, one must turn to the suffering of Christ on the cross. Without a firm grasp of the experience of suffering, Moltmann believes that his hope theology will be incapable of dealing with and overcoming the pain, injury, and ambiguity that one encounters on the road to the earthly New Jerusalem. Moltmann wants his theology of hope to be tougher, more resilient, more capable of enduring disappointments. Therefore, he has crafted a theology of the cross to be the complement to his theology of hope.

It is not necessary here to enter into a detailed discussion of his theology of the cross, which is largely devoted to questions of Christology and the nature of the Trinity. It is sufficient to

note the subtle changes which Moltmann's new emphasis introduces into his theology of hope. For example, we no longer
hear about the God whose mode of existence is the future.
Now Moltmann focuses on the presence of God in Christ. He
argues that when Jesus suffered on the cross not only did he, as
a man, suffer, but (going beyond orthodox Christological for-
mulas once again, but in an opposite—in this case, Patripas-
sian—direction) that God was so very incarnate in Jesus that
God himself suffered too. Here we have an emphatic affirmation of the mode of God's existence as past as well as future.
Also, Moltmann argues that when the murdered and martyred
were suffering at Auschwitz, God was incarnate, suffering along
with them.[146] By implication, wherever people suffer and hurt,
God suffers and hurts too. (This is Moltmann's new approach to
the theodicy problem.) Hence, God's mode of existence can be
thought of as present as well as past and future. Of course,
Moltmann's extreme change of emphasis threatens the uniqueness of God's incarnation in Christ; however, the important
point for our inquiry is that Moltmann has (perhaps unwitting-
ly) moved away from a Gnostic view of God. Although Moltmann can still see this present world as godforsaken, he holds
that even God experiences godforsakenness, and that therefore
where there is godforsakenness (itself a form of suffering) there
is God. And yet, by making God a participant in human suffering and death, Moltmann seems to insert the "actuality of evil"
into God[147]—which is, of course, another familiar Gnostic
theme.

There *is* continuity between Moltmann's hope theology and
his theology of the cross. Although he now recognizes the mis-
placed authority he accorded the Zeitgeist in his early thought,
Moltmann does not recant his heterodox views on Original Sin,
eschatology, or the nature of revelation. But his theology of the
cross is more than a complement to his hope theology. At

points, the one undermines the other. For example, since God is no longer exclusively future, but is present among us now, Moltmann's attitude toward this present world changes. Now we hear Moltmann saying what one would expect an orthodox Christian to say about the world, namely, that "we may not regard this world either as a heaven of self-realization or as a hell of self-alienation. . . . This demands an acceptance of the present situation in spite of its unacceptability. . . ."[148] More generally, the theology of the cross alters the whole tenor and thrust of his thought. He no longer speaks excitedly about the dramatic breaking in of the God of the future, nor of the imperative for man to act now with confidence and freedom, and meet God out on the horizons of human political hopes. The tone is far more sober—even somber.

I would speculate that there may be good reason for the later Moltmann's somber abandonment of hope-full eschatological themes. His contention that God experiences godforsakenness is, to my mind, a textbook case of a contradiction: God = not God. (If this can be explained "dialectically," Moltmann has not shown us how to do it. It is so at odds with the tradition of Christian discourse about God that it cannot be dignified as a necessary paradox.) If Moltmann is serious that God = not God, then how can we be sure—as his hope theology asserted—that the future of man is God? If God = not God, then the future of man may just as well be "not God" as "God." No wonder the later Moltmann is more somber. If God is to be just as "present" in the human future as the later Moltmann says he was in the crucifixion of Jesus, then there is not much reason to look to the future with joy and hope.

In spite of his various changes of emphasis, Moltmann does not wish to depoliticize his "political theology." Indeed, his basic concern is still with correct political action (what he calls "orthopraxy"), not right theological belief ("orthodoxy"). However, his political views are no longer derived from eschatology. Despite some continuity in rhetoric, the political imperative now is not eschatological (humanity going forth into the "open" future to meet God), but ethical (imitation of the suffering Christ who identified with the downtrodden and godforsaken). In the end, his political ethics boil down to a rather routine endorsement of democracy and socialism.[149]

From the point of view of Marxist-Christian convergence, the "new" Moltmann is far less intriguing than the earlier one. He has lost his radical bite. He is more patient, more realistic, more gradualist. But he is not a political conservative by any means. He still looks forward to the revolution of the future. He is still something of a chiliast, for he still hopes for the "human reign of the Son of Man."[150] But he is a chastened chiliast. The revolution is no longer an imminent expectation; it will come, but only "in due time."[151] There is an unfinished quality to his thought. Moltmann is now a dialogical Christian in transition. We shall no doubt hear more from him in the future. If he ever fully shakes himself loose from the Zeitgeist and recovers his Christian roots, one can anticipate that others will take up with the Zeitgeist where he will have left off. The Spirit of the Age is a mighty wind; it bloweth where it listeth.

NOTES

1. Hans Jonas, *The Gnostic Religion,* rev. ed. (Boston: Beacon, 1963), p. 95.
2. Thomas J. J. Altizer, "The Challenge of Modern Gnosticism," *The Journal of Bible and Religion, XXX* (January 1962), p. 22.
3. A. James Gregor, *A Survey of Marxism* (New York: Random House, 1965), p. 109.
4. See Eric Voegelin, *The New Science of Politics* (Chicago: University of Chicago Press, 1952), pp. 106–107.

5. *Ibid.,* p. 122.
6. *Ibid.,* pp. 123–124.
7. *Ibid.,* p. 124.
8. *Ibid.,* p. 126. For an erudite discussion of ancient and modern Gnosticism, see Thomas Molnar, *God and the Knowledge of Reality* (New York: Basic Books, 1973).
9. Ernst Bloch, *Man of His Own* (New York: Herder and Herder, 1970), p. 162. Also see Henri de Lubac, S.J., *The Drama of Atheist Humanism* (Cleveland: World, 1950), p. 195.
10. Voegelin, *op. cit.,* p. 145. Also see Ernst Troeltsch, *The Social Teaching of the Christian Churches* (New York: Harper & Row, 1960), 1: p. 85.
11. Jonas, *op. cit.,* p. 307.
12. Ernst Benz, *Evolution and Christian Hope* (Garden City, N.Y.: Anchor, 1966), p. 39.
13. Norman Cohn, *The Pursuit of the Millennium* (New York: Harper & Row, 1961), p. 101. For an important revisionist view on other aspects of Cohn's classic study, see Robert E. Lerner, *The Heresy of the Free Spirit in the Later Middle Ages* (Berkeley: University of California Press, 1972).
14. Bloch, *op. cit.,* p. 137.
15. *Ibid.*
16. Benz, *op. cit.,* p. 48.
17. *Ibid.*
18. Voegelin, *op. cit.,* p. 111.
19. Cohn, *op. cit.,* p. 101.
20. See Karl Loewith, *Meaning in History* (Chicago: University of Chicago Press, 1949), pp. 208–213.
21. See Charles Reich, *The Greening of America* (New York: Bantam, 1970).
22. Abraham Friesen, *Reformation and Utopia: The Marxist Interpretations of the Reformation and Its Antecedents* (Wiesbaden, West Germany: Franz Steiner, 1974), p. 25. According to Benz, "During the decisive period of his life, Muenzer became acquainted with the writings of Joachim. . . ." (Benz, *op. cit.,* p. 56). Indeed, Muentzer explicitly expressed his indebtedness to Joachist thought. See George H. Williams, *The Radical Reformation* (Philadelphia: Westminster, 1957), pp. 45, 51.

23. Frederick Engels, *The Peasant War in Germany* (New York: International, 1926), p. 65. It is possible that Engels had a vested interest in construing Muentzer as an atheist. See Friesen, *op. cit.,* pp. 237–238.

24. Thomas Muentzer, "Sermon Before the Princes: An Exposition of the Second Chapter of Daniel (Allstedt, July 13, 1524)," *Spiritual and Anabaptist Writers,* George H. Williams and Angel M. Mergal, eds. (Philadelphia: Westminster, 1957), pp. 53, 58, and 61.

25. Eric W. Gritsch, *Reformer Without a Church: The Life and Thought of Thomas Muentzer: 1488 [?]–1525* (Philadelphia: Fortress, 1967), p. 15.

26. Quoted in *ibid.,* p. 93. On the uncertain authenticity of the quote, see p. 93n.

27. Gritsch, *op. cit.,* p. 61. It is worth noting that Gritsch's biography of Muentzer is generally regarded as a sympathetic one.

28. Muentzer, "Sermon Before the Princes," *op. cit.,* pp. 66–67.

29. Roger Garaudy, "What Does a Non-Christian Expect of the Church in Matters of Social Morality?" *The Social Message of the Gospels,* Franz Boeckle, ed. (New York: Paulist, 1968), p. 37.

30. See Grover Foley, "Reaping the Whirlwind," *Cross Currents, XXIII* (Fall 1973), p. 28.

31. See Michael Novak, "Secular Style and Natural Law," *SCD,* p. 83. Recently, Novak has elaborated on his estimate of Cox's promise as follows: "What I meant in my reference to Harvey Cox was that with the *Secular City* he had achieved the public notice both in the religious community and in the general American community that Reinhold Niebuhr had possessed; that gave him a weighty responsibility. Over the years, Cox seems to have lost that stature. He still has considerable power for gaining the attention of the public. The responsibility is still his. It does not seem that he is giving the moral, theological, and intellectual leadership that Reinhold Niebuhr gave, and it may have been unfair to lay so much responsibility upon him. The rules of celebrity have changed since Reinhold Niebuhr's day, and Cox may have been a victim of their vagaries" (letters from Novak to the author, January 5, 1976 and April 29, 1976; printed with permission).

32. Martin E. Marty, "Cox and the Critics," review of *SCD, TCC,*

LXXXIV (January 18, 1967), p. 85. See Martin E. Marty, "Will the Real Harvey Cox Please Stand Up?" *TCC, XCII* (May 28, 1975), p. 559.

33. *SS,* p. 127. Cox, too, stresses the continuity of his thought. See Cox, " 'The Secular City'—Ten Years Later," *TCC, XCII* (May 28, 1975), pp. 544–547.
34. Quoted in Hiley H. Ward, *God and Marx Today* (Philadelphia: Fortress, 1968), p. 65.
35. Cox, "Afterword," *SCD,* p. 193.
36. See *ON,* pp. 16, 37, 141, and *FF,* pp. 87–90.
37. Michael Novak, "The Absolute Future," *New Theology No. 5,* Martin E. Marty and Dean G. Peerman, eds. (New York: Macmillan, 1968), p. 206.
38. Cox, "Non-Theistic Commitment," *Cross Currents, XIX* (Fall 1969), p. 402.
39. *SS,* p. 18. Also see p. 318.
40. Cox, "Feasibility and Fantasy: Sources of Social Transcendence," *The Religious Situation 1969,* Donald R. Cutler, ed. (Boston: Beacon, 1969), p. 920.
41. *SS,* p. 153. J. M. Cameron has perceived *SS* to be a heretical relativization of the Christian message. See J. M. Cameron, "Confusion Among Christians," review of *SS* and other works, *The New York Review of Books, XX* (May 31, 1973), pp. 19–22. For an interesting exchange between Cox and Cameron on the nature of heresy and orthodoxy, see *The New York Review of Books, XX* (September 20, 1973), p. 45.
42. See Cox, "Non-Theistic Commitment," *op. cit.,* p. 403.
43. *SC,* p. 112.
44. *SS,* pp. 75, 152.
45. Reinhold Niebuhr, *The Children of Light and the Children of Darkness* (New York: Scribner's, 1960), p. 135.
46. Cox, "Technology, Modern Man, and the Gospel" (panel discussion with Carl F. H. Henry), *Christianity Today, XII* (July 5, 1968), p. 3.
47. *SC,* p. 98, and Cox, "Afterword," *SCD,* p. 193.
48. *SC,* pp. 1–2.
49. *Ibid.,* p. 111. Although the later Cox surrenders his epochal view of history and his affection for the bureaucratic impersonality

and pragmatic rationality of the city, he does not lose his appreciation of the city as the context of a secular style of life.

50. Cox, "Technology, Modern Man and the Gospel," *op. cit.*, p. 4. Also see Cox, "Afterword," *SCD*, p. 179. Alan L. Mintz sees Cox as "little more than a public-relations official of the *Zeitgeist*, department of religious affairs" [Alan L. Mintz, "Participatory Theology," review of *SS, Commentary, 57* (March 1974), p. 97].

51. Bloch, *op. cit.*, p. 161.

52. See *SC*, p. 66.

53. Will Herberg, *Protestant—Catholic—Jew* (New York: Anchor, 1960), pp. 266–267.

54. *SC*, p. 231. Italics added.

55. *Ibid.*, p. 91.

56. *SS*, p. 153. Italics added.

57. Garaudy, "What Does a Non-Christian Expect of the Church in Matters of Social Morality?" *The Social Message of the Gospels*, Franz Boeckle, ed., pp. 30–31.

58. See *SS*, pp. 232, 311.

59. *GR*, p. 33.

60. *Ibid.*, p. 48.

61. *Ibid.*, pp. 66–67, 68.

62. *Ibid.*, pp. 70, 59. Also see p. 32.

63. *SC*, p. 59.

64. *ON*, pp. 42–43.

65. *SC*, p. 96. Italics added.

66. *Ibid.*, pp. 96–97. Italics in original. And p. 97. Italics added.

67. Cox, "The Biblical Basis of the Geneva Conference," *TCC, LXXXIV* (April 5, 1967), p. 436.

68. Cox, "The Church in East Germany," *Christianity and Crisis, XXIII* (July 22, 1963), p. 139.

69. *ON*, p. 57. Italics added.

70. See above pp. 24–25, see *SC*, pp. 223–225.

71. Cox, "Afterword," *SCD*, p. 203.

72. See *ON*, pp. 12, 88.

73. See Leslie Dewart, *The Future of Belief* (New York: Herder and Herder, 1966). The argument of this book is deepened and amplified in Dewart's later study, *The Foundations of Belief* (New York: Herder and Herder, 1969). However, Cox's indebtedness to

Dewart was based on *The Future of Belief* and expressed before publication of *The Foundations of Belief.*

74. *ON,* p. 88.
75. *Ibid.,* p. 87.
76. *Ibid.,* p. 41.
77. William Hamilton, in "The Spectrum of Protestant Belief," (Robert Campbell, O.P., ed.), *The Sign, 47* (January, 1968), p. 16.
78. *ON,* p. 88.
79. *FF,* p. 156.
80. Cox, "Radical Hope and Empirical Probability," *Christianity and Crisis, XXVIII* (May 31, 1968), p. 98; © copyright 1972 by Christianity and Crisis, Inc.
81. *FF,* p. 87. Italics added. Cox has been quoted as saying that "religion is the most vital revolutionary force we have." See "Dionysus in Boston," *Newsweek, LXXV* (May 11, 1970), p. 77.
82. *SS,* p. 283.
83. *Ibid.,* p. 183.
84. *Ibid.,* p. 66.
85. *Ibid.,* p. 301. Italics added.
86. Cox, "Political Theology for the United States," *Projections: Shaping an American Theology for the Future,* Thomas F. O'Meara and Donald M. Weisser, eds. (Garden City, N.Y.: Image, 1970), p. 50.
87. *ON,* p. 45. Also see *SC,* p. 100.
88. Cox, "Tired Images Transcended: An Interview with Myself," *TCC, LXXXVII* (April 1, 1970), p. 385.
89. See *SC,* pp. 102–103. This resacralization tendency is present in the later Cox as well. Friendly reader Leslie Dewart correctly understands the objective of Cox's *SS* to be "the resacralization of the world" [Leslie Dewart, review of *SS, The Critic, XXXII* (January–February 1974), p. 67].
90. R. A. Knox, *Enthusiasm* (Oxford: Oxford University Press, 1950), p. 3.
91. Roland H. Bainton, "Preface," *Reformer Without a Church: The Life and Thought of Thomas Muentzer: 1488 [?]–1525,* Eric W. Gritsch, p. viii. Lowell H. Zuck has called Muentzer "the ambivalent hero of Protestant theocracy" [L. H. Zuck, "Confession and Recantation: Editor's Note," *Christianity and Revolution: Radical*

Christian Testimonies, 1520–1650, L. H. Zuck, ed. (Philadelphia: Temple University Press, 1975), p. 45].

92. Paul Ramsey, *Who Speaks for the Church?* (New York: Abingdon, 1967), p. 20. In a curious, but cryptic, letter in *Worldview, 18* (February 1975), p. 2, Cox claims that he is not interested in forging a theoretical synthesis of Marxism and Christianity on the basis of the young Marx—or on any basis. Now, he says, he is interested in "the 'scientific' Marx of the more mature writings" and in action—namely, making a socialist revolution in America. Cox has changed his mind in the past; there is no reason why he should not again. It will be interesting to learn more about the reasons for his disillusion with synthetic dialogue, and to learn how he intends to develop his new angle on Marxist-Christian relations.

93. See James A. Taylor, "Giants of Our Faiths," *U.S. Catholic, 39* (December 1974), p. 18.

94. *RRF,* pp. xii, 14. Regarding Moltmann's relation to and reflection on Bloch, particular notice should be taken of Moltmann, "Introduction," Bloch, *op. cit.,* pp. 19–29; Moltmann, "Hope and Confidence: A Conversation with Ernst Bloch," *RRF,* pp. 148–176; Moltmann, "Hope Without Faith: An Eschatological Humanism Without God," *Is God Dead?* Johannes B. Metz, ed. (New York: Paulist, 1966), pp. 25–40; Moltmann, "Ernst Bloch and Hope Without Faith," *EH,* pp. 15–29; Moltmann, "Die Kategorie *Novum* in der christlichen Theologie," *Ernst Bloch zu ehren: Beitraege zu seinem Werk,* Siegfried Unseld, ed. (Frankfurt a. M.: Suhrkamp, 1965), pp. 243–263; and Moltmann, "Messianismus und Marxismus," *Ueber Ernst Bloch: Mit Beitraegen von Martin Walser et al.* (Frankfurt a. M.: Suhrkamp, 1968), pp. 42–60.

95. *Ibid.,* p. 36.

96. Juergen Moltmann, "Man and the Son of Man," *No Man Is Alien: Essays on the Unity of Mankind,* J. Robert Nelson, ed. (Leiden: E. J. Brill, 1971), p. 208. Also see *TH,* p. 286.

97. *Ibid.,* p. 289.

98. *RRF,* pp. 133, 139.

99. *TH,* p. 329.

100. *Ibid.,* pp. 225, 226. Italics added.

101. *HP,* p. 108n.

102. See *RRF*, p. 104.
103. See Moltmann, "Introduction," Bloch, *op. cit.*, pp. 27–28.
104. *RRF*, pp. 5–6. Also see *TH*, p. 294, and Moltmann, "Antwort auf die Kritik der Theologie der Hoffnung," *Diskussion ueber die "Theologie der Hoffnung" von Juergen Moltmann*, Wolf-Dieter Marsch, ed. (Munich: Kaiser, 1967), p. 208.
105. *RRF*, p. 218.
106. *RRF*, p. 220.
107. See *HP*, p. 181.
108. *Ibid.*, p. 183.
109. *Ibid.* Italics added. Rarely does Moltmann come close to resolving his studied ambiguity. The closest he has come is to mention a two-stage view of the relation between revolution and the New Jerusalem: "Christians . . . are perhaps as it were the fools of the revolution. . . . They love it and laugh about it because they are the heralds of an even greater revolution, one in which God will do away with far greater contradictions than those any present revolution can ever have in view. Any world-transforming deed of justice which comes off corresponds to God's justice on earth; and yet it always needs to be referred back to God's own overturning of this world in which even the best cannot be 'very good' " [Moltmann, "The Theology of Revolution," *New Christian* (London), *84* (December 12, 1968), p. 10]. This position has more of an orthodox ring to it; however, it violates the whole rationale of the theology of hope—which is to give man the freedom and responsibility for the salvation or destruction of the world. Furthermore, by separating human action from God's eschatological action, this two-stage conception trivializes political revolutions and disconnects them from the millennial electric circuit from which the theology of hope derives its force and energy in the first place. It is precisely the repeated refusal to distinguish clearly between human freedom and divine action which has given the theology of hope its appeal and its fascination.
110. Moltmann, "Theology as Eschatology," *FH*, pp. 45–47.
111. *Ibid.*, p. 48.
112. Moltmann, *Theology of Play* (New York: Harper & Row, 1972), p. 36.
113. Moltmann, "Theology as Eschatology," *FH*, p. 49. This studied

ambiguity can also be found in the thought of Gustavo Gutiérrez, Latin America's leading dialogical Catholic. See Gustavo Gutiérrez, *A Theology of Liberation* (Maryknoll, N.Y.: Orbis, 1973),
pp. 15, 36–37, 156–160, 177, 227, 231–232. Gutiérrez's thinking is
heavily influenced by Moltmann's.

114. *RRF*, p. 68.
115. *Ibid.*, p. 76.
116. *HP*, p. 107.
117. *RRF*, pp. 80, 17. Moltmann never says whether he believes in life
after death. Clearly, he rejects the Greek notion of the immortality of the soul—as any Christian would—but he is never clear
whether the Christian doctrine of the resurrection of the body in
the life of the world to come really means that God will raise the
dead in glory or whether it is only an existential statement about
the power of love in this life that such a hope can release. See
CG, pp. 166ff.; Moltmann, *Man* (Philadelphia: Fortress, 1974), pp.
57, 102–104; Moltmann, "Eternity," *Listening, 3* (1968), pp. 89–95;
and Moltmann, "Hope Beyond Time," *Duke Divinity School Review, 33* (Spring 1968), pp. 109–114. Traditionally, Christians root
the certainty of their belief in the resurrection of the body after
death in the cornerstone of their faith, namely, the certainty of
Christ's bodily Resurrection. The latter is a given. But Moltmann
reverses this order. He says that the certainty of Christ's Resurrection is to be known in the New Jerusalem—which, unfortunately,
has not yet occurred. Hence, the certainty of Christ's Resurrection is left hanging in the balance. Therefore, it is not surprising
that Moltmann is unclear about whether there will be a new life
beyond death. He has sacrificed the traditional way in which
Christians have rooted their certainty about the resurrected life
after death. See *TH*, p. 190.
118. *HP*, pp. 214, 108.
119. Moltmann, "Theology as Eschatology," *FH*, p. 50.
120. *TH*, p. 337. Also see *EH*, p. 52.
121. See *TH*, p. 337.
122. Walter H. Capps, "Mapping the Hope Movement," *The Future of
Hope*, Capps, ed. (Philadelphia: Fortress, 1970), p. 39.
123. *TH*, p. 16. For ambiguous qualifications of this assertion, see *EH*,
pp. 50–52.
124. Rosemary Radford Ruether, *The Radical Kingdom: The Western*

Experience of Messianic Hope (New York: Harper & Row, 1970), p. 217.

125. "Theology as Eschatology," FH, p. 10.

126. Langdon Gilkey, "The Universal and Immediate Presence of God," ibid., p. 84.

127. Martin E. Marty and Dean G. Peerman, "Christian Hope and Human Futures," New Theology No. 5, Marty and Peerman, eds. (New York: Macmillan, 1968), pp. 17–18.

128. TH, p. 190.

129. Ibid., pp. 325–326.

130. Alasdair MacIntyre, "The Debate about God: Victorian Relevance and Contemporary Irrelevance," The Religious Significance of Atheism, Alasdair MacIntyre and Paul Ricoeur (New York: Columbia University Press, 1969), pp. 22–23.

131. See RRF, p. 61.

132. Ibid., p. 62. Perhaps Moltmann's appropriation of the concept of hope is simply misleading and irresponsible. At points he equates hope with openness to the future: "Hoping does not mean to have a number of hopes at one's disposal. It means, rather, hoping to be open" (EH, p. 20).

133. HP, pp. 194, 82.

134. TH, p. 92.

135. EH, p. 6.

136. Moltmann, "The Future as Threat and as Opportunity," The Religious Situation 1969, Cutler, ed., p. 934.

137. Moltmann, "Die Revolution der Freiheit," Perspektiven der Theologie: Gesammelte Aufsaetze (Munich: Kaiser, and Mainz: Matthias-Gruenewald, 1968), p. 193 (the translation is mine). A shorter and somewhat different version of this essay was delivered by Moltmann as a speech and translated into English in RRF, pp. 63–82. The quotation from the German edition does not appear in the English translation.

138. Langdon Gilkey, "The Contribution of Culture to the Reign of God," The Future as the Presence of Shared Hope, Maryellen Muckenhirn, ed. (New York: Sheed and Ward, 1968), pp. 39–42.

139. See Walter Niggs, The Heretics (New York: Knopf, 1962), p. 31. One of Moltmann's fellow dialogical Christians, Rubém Alves, a Latin American, contends that since Moltmann's God is so ahis-

torical, Moltmann has fallen into Docetism—a heretical Christo-logical position that has affinities with Gnosticism. Rubém A. Alves, *A Theology of Human Hope* (St. Meinrad, Ind.: Abbey, 1969), p. 94.

140. See Gilkey, "The Contribution of Culture to the Reign of God," *The Future as the Presence of Shared Hope*, pp. 54–55. For evidence that Moltmann has become uncomfortable with these implications, see Moltmann, *Theology of Play*, pp. 23, 48, and *EH*, pp. 101–118. I have never noticed an urge on Moltmann's part to make man into a god, although his susceptibility to theocracy and Gnostic redivinization of the world push him in that direction.

141. Moltmann, "Theology as Eschatology," *FH*, p. 14.

142. Bloch, *op. cit.,* p. 164.

143. *AD*, p. 95.

144. Moltmann, "Response to the Opening Presentations," *Hope and the Future of Man*, Ewert H. Cousins, ed. (Philadelphia: Fortress, 1972), p. 90.

145. *CG*, p. 11.

146. *Ibid.*, p. 278. Also see *EH*, p. 73.

147. See Carl E. Braaten, "A Trinitarian Theology of the Cross," review of *CG*, *The Journal of Religion, 56* (January 1976), p. 119.

148. Moltmann, *Man*, p. 36.

149. See *CG*, pp. 11, 63, 317–338, and Moltmann, "The Cross and Civil Religion," *Religion and Political Society*, The Institute of Christian Thought, ed. (New York: Harper & Row, 1974), pp. 14–46.

150. Moltmann, *Man*, p. 116.

151. *CG*, p. 5.

4

Toward Understanding
Dialogical Marxism

Either we destroy Revisionism or
Revisionism will destroy us. . . .

MOSKVA (SOVIET MAGAZINE), 1958

THE SPECTER OF REVISIONISM

Revisionism is a deviation from normative Marxism in a rightward direction. Marxist-Leninists usually understand revisionism to be synonymous with "right-wing opportunism." (There is
also a left-wing deviation, but this is of negligible importance to
the dialogue in Europe and North America, which is the context
of our inquiry.) In the Western world, revisionism is understood
to be that which undermines the vital interests of the Soviet

Communist Party (which interests are supposed to be broadly equivalent to the interests of the international workers' movement and all socialist societies). But who decides what undermines the vital interests of the Party? The leadership of the Party decides. The Party also takes upon itself the task of distinguishing a "creative" development of Marxism (which is how Lenin's revision of classical Marxism is understood) from a regressive or revisionist development.

Revisionists frequently charge that orthodox Communists are "dogmatists," unwilling to apply Marxist analysis to new situations. This is a fallacy since orthodox Communists, not the least Joseph Stalin, have made their share of doctrinal innovations. The critical point is that *"legitimate" doctrinal development takes place under the auspices of the Party.* Outside the Party, it is likely to be revisionist; inside the Party, "creative." (Analogously, within Christianity, "legitimate" doctrinal development takes place under the auspices of tradition, outside of which it is likely to be heterodox.) This may sound capricious and perhaps cynical, but I would argue that—given Marxist-Leninist presuppositions—it is not. The Communist seeks to make socialist revolution and then construct a flawless communist society on a worldwide scale. But socialist revolution cannot be achieved without scientific knowledge, because without such knowledge one will forever be bogged down in the quagmire of utopianism, in the morass of good—but fruitless—intentions. The Party is the guardian of such knowledge. Thus, it holds the key to the secrets of the future—both the secrets of when and how to make revolution, and how to construct communism. Hence, to undermine the Party is to undermine the future. If the Party has privileged insight into the future, the Party is eminently qualified to determine what it is that would undermine itself.

Hence, an indispensable characteristic of all socialist societies (which is what Marxist-Leninists call their current societies) is the monopolistic and vanguard role of the Party. Whatever disputes there may be between various socialist societies, as long as the role of the Party (armed with correct theory) is affirmed, socialism is ultimately secure. As is shown below, the deterioration of the role of the Czechoslovak Communist Party in 1968 was a major cause of the Soviet invasion.

The quintessence of revisionism is social democratization. According to Leopold Labedz, most of the East European revisionists "arrived at some sort of social-democratic position."[1] Social Democracy is the arch rival of Communism in the world proletarian movement. Although Social Democrats are not counterrevolutionaries, they are potentially more dangerous than counterrevolutionaries because they would, so to speak, "deceive the very elect." That is, by distracting the workers with the promise of petty reforms, they divert the workers from fulfilling their historical destiny, which is total revolution. By robbing the workers of their class consciousness and the will to revolution, they prolong the agony of capitalism indefinitely.

The trouble with the Social Democrats is that they are pluralists (or Western-style democrats). There is no room in their theory for one-party dictatorship. Also, because of their defensive unwillingness to offend the bourgeoisie, they never get around to nationalizing all the means of production (which—along with the monopolistic and vanguard role of the Party—constitutes the Soviet definition of socialism). The Soviets can point with justification to the fact that no Social Democratic party has ever liquidated capitalism—that is, an economy based on the private ownership of productive property. The Soviets contend that Social Democrats covertly aid and abet the class enemy.

Once socialism has been established, social democratizing or revisionist trends always take the form of attempts to undo the dictatorship of the Party, which in turn would make the social system vulnerable to imperialistic adventures and capitalistic revivals, and frustrate all hope for full-blown communism. Hence, orthodoxy and revisionism are ultimately mortal enemies. Revisionism is not a mere refinement of Soviet Marxism, but its very denial.

In spite of what may seem to be the haphazard way in which Marxism-Leninism has come into existence, the ideology itself manifests a coherent and interrelated structure. Moreover, it claims for itself the mantle of absolute truth. Hence, to question a basic premise threatens to destroy the entire system of thought.

Historical determinism is probably the basic premise of Marxism. That there is a good measure of economic necessity in the transition from capitalism to socialism is what sets Marxism apart from utopian socialism and enables it to refer to itself as scientific socialism. Much of the revisionist enthusiasm for the *young* Marx derives from a desire to find an *in*determinist or "humanistic" kind of socialism. Those who seek to develop Marxism in this direction usually find themselves at odds not only with Stalin, but with Lenin, Engels, and the mature Marx, that is, with the normative Marxist tradition (Marxism-Leninism). In the words of A. James Gregor, "It is difficult to know how far such a development can proceed without precipitating tensions within Marxism-Leninism of such an order that the *fundamental theoretical structure* of the system would be jeopardized."[2]

So far as the dialogue is concerned, another important issue is the extent to which atheism is an integral part of Marxism. Neutrality or indifference toward religion is a distinguishing mark of Social Democracy. Below I argue that for Communism to abandon its compulsory atheism would be, in the words of Helmut Gollwitzer, "an expression of the profoundest change. . . ."[3] After that, I proceed to a discussion of the indeterminism of the young Marx, and then to a discussion of the role of the Party in Marxism-Leninism.

MARXISM AND ATHEISM

One of the vital issues in the dialogue is the allegedly atheist character of Marxism. The key question is whether atheism is an intrinsic part of the Marxist world view and the Communist movement. This is a poignant question because Marxism has historically not only been atheistic, but has been perceived by outsiders to be something of a counterchurch, and an ersatz religion. This "religious" way of interpreting Marxism has been ventilated so frequently, however, that to comment further might indeed be trite, as Alasdair MacIntyre has suggested.[4] Suffice it to say that Marxism is a "religious" phenomenon in the sense that it demands "unconditional commitment"[5] and taps religious energies. I will argue that the atheism of Marxism is not only intrinsic but related to the "religious" quality of the world view.

The starting point of Marx's atheism was the imperative that man be the supreme being for man.[6] Marx's "world-conquering" philosophy proclaimed that man's consciousness is the "supreme divinity. There must be no god on level with it."[7] Ludwig Feuerbach held that God was nothing but the projection of man's highest qualities into an alien realm. This projection impoverished man, hence, Feuerbach called on man to retrieve that projection. The result would be the deification of man. Marx drew on Feuerbach's insight and held that man and history would be radically transformed when, in Voegelin's words, "man draws his projection back into himself, when he becomes conscious that he himself is God. . . ."[8]

When the subject of Marx's atheism is raised, the Marxian dictum that "religion is the opium of the people" most frequently comes to mind. Some Christians assume that if Christians were to promote rather than impede the social liberation of humanity, then Marxists would no longer have any justification for their atheism. This assumption is erroneous because Marx's atheism was much more profound. Ultimately, it was based on his theory of action. That is, fundamentally, Marx was an atheist not merely because religion kept people poor and economically enslaved, but because religion subordinated man to a creator-God, thereby denying man's full dignity, independence, and freedom of action.[9] Human freedom, autonomy, and self-creation were categorical imperatives prior to rational argument for Marx, especially the young Marx. In the words of the young Marx: "A being does not regard himself as independent unless he is his own master, and he is only his own master when he owes his existence to himself. . . . But I live completely by another person's favor when I owe to him not only the continuance of my life but also its *creation;* when he is its *source.*"[10] Hence, God is not merely an irrelevancy (implying agnosticism or a bland atheism), but an obstacle (implying militant atheism) to human freedom and self-liberation.

Marx considered Prometheus "the noblest of saints and martyrs in the calendar of philosophy." Because Marx regarded atheism as the precondition for freedom and wanted man to be the supreme being, he could approvingly quote Prometheus's defiant words: "I shall never exchange my fetters for slavish servility. 'Tis better to be chained to the rock than bound to the service of Zeus.' "[11] Marx's primary motive for denying the creator-God was not scientific evidence or philosophical reasoning, but the imperative that man be both free and godlike. Marx not only wanted to free man from the gods but to dethrone gods and grant their powers to man.

Marx's atheism was unequivocal. It was his youthful stress on human autonomy that stimulated dialogical Christians to place such a strong emphasis of their own on human autonomy. Manuel Azcárate, a Spanish Communist and former colleague of Garaudy's at the Center for Marxist Research and Studies in Paris, has said that a religion "that confirms the role of man as creator of his own history" removes the philosophical obstacles to dialogue.[12] We have seen, however, that dialogical Christians cannot affirm man's self-sufficient autonomy without falling into heresy and defining "God" so that he ultimately dies a death of a thousand qualifications.

Marx said that, "For Germany the *criticism of religion* is in the main complete, and criticism of religion is the premise of all criticism."[13] Without the criticism of religion there could be no criticism of politics. When religion is debunked, man realizes that he is in fact free, free to fulfill his Promethean mission. Man no longer has any justification for resigning himself to the fake remedies of theology, the opiates of religion. Said Marx: "The criticism of religion disillusions man to make him think and act and shape his reality like a man who has been disillusioned. . . ."[14] Likewise, the rejection of religion entails the rejection of a debased social condition which requires just such a bogus solution. Hence, the criticism of religion is not only the beginning, but the catalyst of all criticism.

But the denial of the world and that world's God go hand in hand. Marxism stands in the Gnostic tradition, rejecting as it does the world of the present, the alleged goodness of that world, and the God who allegedly created and sustains that world. The world, Marx said, is a *"vale of woe"* and religion is its *"halo."*[15] Even if there were a God he would have to be an evil God to have created and sustained such a wretched world. Hence, one cannot repudiate the world without repudiating its God; likewise, one cannot renounce God without renouncing his world.

Even though certain Marxists may today be friendly to religion, historically Marxism had to be antireligious. If religion diverted people from perceiving the real nature of their problems and acting upon those perceptions, religion first had to be attacked and discredited. Historically the Marxist movement did engage in antireligious education and agitation. But Marxists were free to engage in other activities because, as Marx pointed out, the criticism of religion was already largely accomplished.

Secularization has continued to progress to the point where today many Marxists feel free to eschew militant atheism altogether. The religious mentality is generally no longer a massive obstacle to the advance of Communism in Europe. There are pockets of potential religious resistance, but they can perhaps be neutralized substantially by means of dialogue and assurance of a hands-off policy toward religion should Communists assume power. Hence, the transition to socialism can be accelerated and accomplished more smoothly. This approach harmonizes well with the strategy of peaceful and parliamentary transition to socialism now being practiced in Western Europe.[16]

Another factor facilitating a more tolerant approach to religion is the rise of a modernist and social welfare Christianity in certain Christian circles, wherein the Marxist critique of religion has already been largely absorbed and applied. In such situations the difference between Marxists and Christians is not so much substantive as it is rhetorical and symbolic. Marxists correctly see in these Christians potential allies. It is a minor sacrifice for Marxists to suspend open atheism in order to avoid offending the residual religious sentiments of these people.

Left-wing Christians, however, may not be reliable allies. Some of them carry around lingering, perhaps nostalgic, proclivities for personal immortality and an eternal salvation beyond history. Some of them say the Kingdom is always just arriving; hence, the ideal society is forever receding beyond the horizon. When the social struggle demands absolute and sustained commitment, these attitudes can encourage passivity. Therefore, although Marxists may make alliance with leftist Christians they cannot compromise the atheist character of their own ideology. To do so would sap the motivating power of the ideology and weaken the will for total secular salvation. Furthermore, left-wing Christians like Cox and Moltmann have a bizarre tendency to build their social theories around myths rather than on scientific socialism. Georges Sorel took a similar approach to social change. He began his career as a Marxist and ended it as a crypto-fascist. Marxists would want to ask if people so beholden to myths can really be trusted.

Marx and Engels did not bother to frame a sustained, systematic argument against the validity of religion. They had other preoccupations. They wanted to free man for self-creation and self-redemption. As Louis Dupré put it: "Marx's own negative attitude toward religion was never based upon speculative arguments for the non-existence of God. He rejected religion because it was incompatible with his theory of action."[17] (Unfortunately, the mature Marx compromised his own theory of action when he began to talk in terms of inevitability, iron necessity, and historical laws. Nevertheless, neither Marx nor the Marxists were ever to equivocate on the question of God.) Marx and Engels did not feel it was necessary to make the intellectual case against religion because they assumed the case had already been made by Feuerbach and the eighteenth century bourgeois atheists. Furthermore, their theory of historical materialism, whereby economics is the ultimate independent variable or causal factor in history, undermined any claim to absolute truth that a religion could make. Finally, by employing a biblical criterion ("Ye shall know them by their fruits") they could see in religion and the churches only the perpetuation of human misery and degradation. This was not the cause of their atheism, but only the proof of the pudding, so to speak. In sum, there can be no doubt that Marx and Engels were atheists who regarded religion as a definite evil, and that no religious belief can be reconciled with classical Marxism.

I have alluded to the fact that Marxism's Promethean atheism is indispensable to its revolutionary energy and dynamism, its messianism. But much as secular messianism requires atheism, so atheism implies secular messiansim; for without a God man *must* find and make his own salvation if he is to avoid despair and defeat. According to Gollwitzer, "Communism will maintain atheism as long as it remains messianic."[18] Conversely, Communism will be messianic as long as it remains militantly atheistic. Both messianism and atheism are inextricably bound up with the nature of Marxism-Leninism.

It is not my intention to rehearse all the reasons why the Marxist-Leninist *movement* (especially when in power) is atheistic and aggressively antireligious. Suffice it to say that were Communism to abandon its atheistic and apocalyptic messianism, it would mean that it had transformed itself into Social Democracy, which is neither messianic, apocalyptic, nor officially atheistic. Gollwitzer has speculated on what factors might promote the severing of Communism from its atheistic messianism. He has cited "the sobering effect of the gradual realization of the social revolution, the influence of old and new social conditions, the experience of the immutability of human nature and the insoluble and unchangeable uncertainties of human life."[19] In other words, Communism will surrender its atheistic messianism when it loses its self-confidence, its militant optimism, its eschatological vision, and its ability to mobilize masses of people—that is, when it imitates Social Democracy. In addition, under these circumstances Communist societies would probably be unable to sustain their character as mobilization systems and hence to justify their "totalitarian" institutions. They would either devolve into an ossified authoritarianism and/or quasi-democratic pluralism. Therefore, just as atheism is necessary to Marx's theory of action, so it is necessary to the motivational and institutional character of modern Marxism-Leninism. The indulgent attitude toward religion fostered by dialogical Marxists poses a subtle threat to the very essence of Marxism-Leninism.

MARXISM-LENINISM AND THE INDETERMINISM OF
THE YOUNG MARX

The wide dissemination of the writings of the young Marx, which occurred only after the Second World War, facilitated the possibility of a Marxist-Christian dialogue. Christians who found Marx appealing usually directed their interest to the young Marx because of his alleged "spiritual existentialism" and "rational mysticism."[20] Yes, the young Marx was an uncompromising atheist; however, his atheism—when compared to that of the older Marx—was perceived to be inspired by clearly ethical, even vaguely "religious," concerns. It was also thought that the early Marx was an *in*determinist and antiauthoritarian, hence more compatible with liberal, Western ideas of freedom and democracy. Thus, those Marxists interested in dialogue with Christians (as well as with existentialists) found in the young Marx a convenient medium for communication.

It is significant that preoccupation with the young Marx has been more characteristic of the international New Left than of any other political or ideological current. As such, it is not surprising that the dialogue reflects many of the influences found in the secular New Left.

There has been a great deal of controversy concerning the young Marx in Marxist and radical circles (not to mention exclusively scholarly circles). How one stands on the interpretation of the young Marx has become a litmus test for revisionism. According to the orthodox Soviet view, the young Marx was a romantic aberration from the normative Marxism of the mature Marx (and there is evidence that this is exactly how the mature Marx and Engels themselves regarded the matter[21]). In the words of Louis Althusser, the arch rival of Garaudy (when Garaudy was still in the French Party), "Marx's Early Works have been a war-horse for petty bourgeois intellectuals in their struggle against Marxism. . . ." The interest in the young Marx, he charges, is promoted by revisionist Communist intellectuals and is related to Communist dialogue with Christians. For Althusser, the young Marx was a "pre-Marxist idealist" whereas the mature Marx was "scientific."[22]

On the other side, the issue was joined by a leading American social democrat, Michael Harrington, who charged: "The Communists could not tolerate the integration of the Manuscripts [of the young Marx] into the Marxian canon, for that would subvert their elitist and mechanistic interpretation of Marx."[23]

What Althusser and Harrington—and many others—say indicates that the young Marx and the older Marx may represent two distinct political philosophies. Orthodox Marxists generally dismiss the young Marx, whereas those sympathetic to the young Marx (sometimes called "neo-Marxists") regard the young Marx as the authentic Marx and interpret the mature Marx (who is too monumental simply to dismiss) in terms of the young Marx, or else argue that the young Marx and the older Marx actually represent a single organic philosophy. Although I find the Soviet interpretation of Marxism more credible than the neo-Marxist ones, it is not my purpose to rebut the neo-Marxist views in this book. What follows is simply a sketch of the orthodox interpretation and a statement of the differences between neo-Marxism and Soviet-style Marxism centering on the issue of freedom and determinism. In Chapter 5 on Roger

Garaudy, I analyze one neo-Marxist's failed attempt to blur the differences between the young Marx and normative Marxism.

The central concern of the young Marx was *Entfremdung,* that is, alienation (significantly, the preoccupation of existentialism as well). Alienation is heteronomy, the subservience of man to an external reality he has made but which he does not recognize as his own. If heteronomy or human dependence on outside forces is the problem, then obviously the solution is autonomy or human self-creation. Given this solution, it stands to reason that there is a preference for environmental *in*determinism over determinism to be found in the young Marx. The young Marx's theory of action requires that man—not God, not history, but human beings—be free to determine the undetermined.

The mature Marx identified the main problem as economic exploitation. He identified liberation with the social ownership of the means of production. However, for the young Marx the main problem was alienation, a much broader concept which can be understood to include private property, class division, money, poor conditions of labor, machinery, the state, the commodity market, the division of labor, and religion. The social ownership of the means of production was not an end in itself, but only one of the necessary instruments for achieving the ethical end of disalienation or human self-fulfillment.

The criteria of value for the young Marx were man as a species being and man as an individual, whereas for the mature Marx the criteria were history and economic class. For the young Marx, the history of mankind was not so much the history of class struggle as the history of man's self-alienation through the reification of the products of his labor (as well as the products of his brain, as in religion). Alienation entails reification, that is, the turning of human artifacts into oppressive fetishes or idols. But for the mature Marx, history was less a product of human self-alienation than it was of economic necessity and class struggle. The mature Marx tended to subordinate man to the economic laws of history, thus undermining human freedom and responsibility, much as he had originally accused religion of doing.

The Marxism of the mature Marx is to a significant degree deterministic in an economic sense. As Gregor has said of classical Marxism: "The productive forces are usually spoken of in an active sense . . . and human beings, although energized agents, remain passive in the sense that initiative somehow rests with the productive forces." Marx and Engels were convinced that there were "*necessary* and *inevitable* laws which history pursued and which permitted them to make predictions with 'mathematical certainty.' "[24]

However, in 1890, toward the end of his life (and after Marx had died), Engels seemingly revised this determinism in a letter to Joseph Bloch. Engels asserted that the economic factor was not the only determining element, but merely the *ultimately* determining one. "The economic situation is the basis, but the various elements of the superstructure [most generally: ideas] . . . also exercise their influence upon the course of the historical struggles and in many cases preponderate in determining their *form.*"[25] Engels claimed that this was what he and Marx had meant all along, although they had not found the opportunity to say as much before.

What is at issue here is whether human action is determined by historical laws; in particular, whether human thought is determined by economic forces. In the abstract, the question is analogous to the one dialogical Christians have wrestled with, namely, whether or to what extent people are free to determine their destiny.

There is no doubt that Engels's appendix to classical Marxism sounded a new note; however, it can be argued quite plausibly that Engels (just as he said) was clarifying Marxism more than altering it. Indeed, it is generally agreed that Marx never was a "vulgar" or mechanistic materialist and did not absolutely deny man a role in the making of history. For example, in his "Theses on Feuerbach," Marx said: "The materialist doctrine that men are products of circumstances and upbringing, and that, therefore, changed men are products of other circumstances and changed upbringing, forgets that it is men that change circumstances, and that the educator himself needs educating."[26] From a different angle, but in a similar vein (in "The Eighteenth Brumaire of Louis Bonaparte"), he said: "Men make their own history, but they do not make it just as they please; they do not make it under circumstances chosen by themselves, but under circumstances directly encountered, given and transmitted from the past."[27] What Marx said here is not unlike what Engels said in his letter to Bloch: "We make our history ourselves, but, in the first place, under very definite assumptions and conditions. Among these the economic ones are ultimately decisive."[28]

Although the main burden of classical Marxism is deterministic, it is also true that there is an element of ambiguity on the question of whether man is the creature or the creator of history. This ambiguity has encouraged neo-Marxists to *develop* Marxism in an indeterminist or voluntarist direction.

According to the determinist view, the revolution will occur inevitably. Since men must want to make revolution in order that there can be revolution, the determinist view holds that the workers acquire revolutionary consciousness spontaneously, that is, as an inevitable consequence of their living and working conditions. This view is in a sense "democratic," since the masses make the revolution without the need of mediation by a self-appointed vanguard elite.

Lenin sharply repudiated this notion of spontaneity. He argued that when the workers are left to their own devices the only consciousness they can generate is a "trade union consciousness," that is, a bourgeois reformist mentality. Authentic revolutionary consciousness can only be injected from outside, that is, from intellectuals (in most cases of bourgeois origin). This is a curious inversion of Marx's economic determinism, which holds that *being* (or economic and social conditions) *determines consciousness.* According to Lenin, proletarian conditions produce not revolutionary proletarian consciousness, but bourgeois consciousness. Moreover, in significant cases, bourgeois conditions can yield not bourgeois consciousness, but revolutionary proletarian consciousness.

Some dialogical Marxists like Garaudy, anxious to affirm abstract human freedom *and* their Leninist credentials in the face of Party criticism, have hastily concluded that Lenin, supposedly like the young Marx, was an indeterminist. In fact, Lenin was not an indeterminist. He did not argue that revolution could be made regardless of the social and economic conditions. Rather, he strongly affirmed the lawful character of historical development, and insisted that revolution could be made only when the conditions were right. However, what Lenin was driving at was that only professional revolutionary intellectuals (at the helm of the revolutionary Party) could grasp the scientific socialist understanding of history; of this the working masses were incapable. Since revolutionary practice was impossible without revolutionary theory, the workers left to themselves could not make revolution, even under revolutionary conditions. Actually, Lenin came to justify this stand on economic determinist grounds in his subsequent theory of imperialism. He argued that the workers of metropolitan Europe were bought off by capitalists who, because of the superprofits they extracted from their colonies, were able to satisfy the immediate demands of their workers for better working conditions and higher standards of living. The idea that the workers' movement might be led by bourgeois intellectuals had ample precedent in Marx and Engels themselves, who were nonproletarian intellectuals obsessively anxious to insure that the workers' movement was armed with correct Marxian consciousness.

Actually, Lenin was not affirming abstract human freedom at the expense of determinism any more than the mature Marx was. Rather, he was spelling out one of history's most compelling arguments for dictatorship. In Lenin's hands, the Marxian concept of *praxis* or human freedom (which was part and parcel of the young Marx's theory of action) was lodged in the agency of the vanguard Party. For Lenin, *praxis* became *partiinost*—or "Party-mindedness," which means that truth and goodness are whatever serves the active, conscious agency serving the proletariat in its struggle, that is, whatever serves the vanguard Party. It was axiomatic for Lenin that the masses do not know what is in their own best interests; only the Party, which has privileged insight into the profundities of historical necessity, knows what is in the best interests of the masses; only the Party is the vehicle of true proletarian consciousness. Since freedom is not an abstract imperative, but the recognition of necessity, and since only the Party knows of what necessity consists, true freedom can be guaranteed only by advancing the interests of the Party (as defined by the Party), that is, by obeying the directives of the Party.

Hence, Lenin was a radical voluntarist and, simultaneously, a radical determinist. Lenin's combination of these two positions is not contradictory, but a uniquely persuasive formula for dictatorship. Actually, in this case radical voluntarism is encouraged by radical determinism. This is so because the great masses are viewed as being benighted *and* conditioned, only capable of liberation under the guidance of the enlightened few who possess special knowledge of historical processes and special competence in handling those processes.[29]

Lenin's "voluntarism" comes no closer to affirming the autonomy and free creativity of the human individual than does Marx's "determinism." The mature Marx subordinated the individual to the dictates of history and the imperatives of class. Within limits man makes history, but as an aggregate, as a class, not as an individual. Lenin retains the dictates of history while elevating the imperatives of class into the imperatives of the Party (and after the revolution, the Party-state), which is the vanguard of the working class. The ambiguity in classical Marxism as to whether man is the creature or the creator of history is credibly clarified (in at least one way) by Lenin. The masses of mankind (including the workers) are the creatures of history; however, the select people who compose (the leadership of) the Party are, within limits, the creators of history. When the Party perceives that the objective conditions are ripe and revolution is possible, the "subjective" moment arises wherein the initiative of the Party is all-important. The Promethean mission that the young Marx ascribed to mankind in general was vested by Lenin in the Party elite. Hence, the alleged similarity between the voluntarism of Lenin and the young Marx is superficial and illusory. Whereas the criteria of value for the young Marx were man in general and the individual in particular, the criteria of value for the mature Marx were history and class, and for Lenin, history and class (as represented by the omnicompetent Party). Moreover, in both the mature Marx and in Lenin voluntarism is balanced with a generous dose of determinism. In the young Marx man is free to create history, whereas in the older Marx man is "free" only when conforming himself to the true consciousness which is the recognition of historical necessity. Similarly, in Lenin man is "free" only when conforming

himself to the will of the Party, which is the vessel of true consciousness and the authoritative interpreter of historical necessity. Obviously, then, there is much more congruity between
the mature Marx and Lenin than between the young Marx and
Lenin.

But to the neo-Marxist, the Leninist Party is a reification, a
new master. It denies man his freedom and self-determination;
it alienates him. Such a Party dominates man; man does not and
cannot control such a Party.

According to the Soviet view, man is only "fully man" and
mature under full-blown communism. In the meantime man is
"still immature, still being formed. And he is treated accordingly
by the party. . . . The result . . . is paternalism." Hence, man is
not "capable of choosing his own ends and assuming responsibility for his decisions." Hence, man has only extrinsic, not intrinsic, worth. "At best he is a brick of the social building.
. . ."[30] The neo-Marxists want to get away from this paternalis-
tic Party-mindedness. They tend to argue that man is and can be
(right now) more mature and responsible than the Party dare
imagine. In fact, the heavy-handedness of the Party keeps man
in an artificial state of dependence and helplessness. Instead of
helping man overcome his alienation, the Party intensifies it.
The neo-Marxists want to say that man has "come of age" and
can be trusted with freedom and a democratic form of socialism.

According to official doctrine, only under pure communism
will man be mature, and hence capable of bearing the burden
of freedom. However (assuming freedom is defined as the general absence of external restraints), it is actually a limited freedom. Man under communism will be so thoroughly socialized
that all of the external restraints formerly imposed by the state
will be either internalized or enshrined in group pressure. "Paradoxically, he will be so completely trained in what he should

do that he will have neither the impetus nor motive for acting other than as he should. . . ."[31]

For the young Marx, wherever man revolves around a reification instead of revolving around himself, he is alienated. When alienation, not economic exploitation (which is only one aspect of alienation), is defined as *the* problem, then the solution is phrased in terms of freedom, creativity, and self-determination, rather than social ownership of the means of production. The result must be a highly democratic and libertarian philosophy where one-party dictatorship, censorship, and indoctrination are seen as alienating perversions of Marxism. According to Erich Fromm, another American social democrat, the young Marx "clearly excludes a concept of socialism in which man is manipulated by a bureaucracy. . . . It means that the individual participates actively in the planning *and* in the execution of the plans; it means, in short, the realization of political and industrial democracy."[32] Thus, the young Marx is radically incompatible with the structure of power in Communist countries in general and with the dictatorship of the Party in particular. In fact, intellectuals in Eastern Europe have used the young Marx as a philosophical weapon (a "war-horse," to recall Althusser's words) against the Party and the power structure.

The mature Marx dropped the term "alienation," but essentially equated it with private ownership of productive property. Thus, the liberation of humanity was identified with the expropriation of private property. The Soviet Marxists adopted this position, arguing that under socialism there could be, by definition, no exploitation or alienation. Since exploitation was a class phenomenon and the Soviet Union was a classless society, there could be no exploitation. The state bureaucracy could not be exploitative because, according to Marxist theory, political power was only a reflex of economic power. Since economic power was in the hands of the people, political power reinforced, rather than undermined, that fact. Although the mature Marx also mentioned the division of labor as an alienating factor, the Soviet Marxists have seen no problem here either. They recognize that the division of labor persists; however, under socialist conditions it is not regarded as alienating. In general, the Soviets contend that what little alienation there may be in socialist societies is due to bourgeois survivals and influences from the West.

The neo-Marxists, on the other hand, claim that old forms of alienation persist (class division, "private" ownership by the managerial class, the division of labor, money, the market, and machinery) while new forms have arisen (the socialist state bureaucracy and ruling stratum with their attendant status and privileges). According to Mihailo Markovíc, a Yugoslav neo-Marxist, some old forms of alienation have survived while "new unsuspected ones have appeared" because of the "enormous power" lodged in "unlimited political authority." As examples, he has cited "new forms of political oppression introduced by bureaucracy; new ways of grabbing the surplus product, even without possessing the means of production; new tensions between rich and poor; new conflicts between nations and countries within the socialist camp, etc." He also warns about the alienating potential of technology, which despite its material benefits sometimes makes man "a slave of his own products" and "increases his spiritual poverty."[33]

Generally, the neo-Marxists have such a broad conception of alienation that they tend to see it almost everywhere. Sometimes the concept seems to function roughly as a synonym for imperfection. The practical consequence of this is to blunt the struggle for social salvation. For example, Bronislaw Baczko, a Polish revisionist has said: "Emancipation from alienation is not for Marxism a final state—but a process."[34] A Yugoslav revisionist, Danilo Pejović, has said: "The goal of history, the full sense of history, can never be realized in its totality. We can only approach it more closely."[35]

I would speculate that people will fight, struggle, and sacrifice on a sustained basis for the Kingdom of God on earth, for communism, for a Sorelian general strike, for some apocalyptic denouement, but their imagination cannot so easily be engaged by the promise of an eternal process where the final goal is ever receding over the horizon. Communist polities are mobilization systems requiring a black-and-white view of the world. Revisionism, by pointing the finger of criticism inward, obfuscates the issue between socialism and capitalism, between "good" and "evil." It enfeebles the driving power of Marxist ideology and undercuts its sense of urgency and discipline about politics. Revisionism—however correct its analysis of alienation in socialist societies may be—introduces the "disease" of self-doubt into the Marxist-Leninist movement. Revisionism not only impugns the ideological character and institutional manifestations of the movement, but also undermines the militant and dynamic nature of its psychology.

THE MARXIST-LENINIST PARTY: THE CASE OF CZECHOSLOVAKIA IN 1968

Revisionist or social democratizing tendencies were clearly manifest in Czechoslovakia in the spring of 1968. These tendencies culminated in an assault on the monopoly and vanguard role of the Party, which, in Soviet eyes, was tantamount to an assault on socialism itself. The invasion by the Soviet Union and other Warsaw Pact powers immediately followed.

According to Jan M. Lochman, a Czechoslovak theologian, there are two versions of Marxism. The first is that of the mature Marx, Engels, Lenin, and Stalin. According to this version, history is a determined process and freedom is the recognition of necessity. "History is in this sense the extension and extrapolation of reason; so that if you have the right philosophy, then you possess all the solutions. That's the danger." The other version is that of the young Marx, whose starting point was his theory of action, according to which "one does not have all the solutions, so to say, beforehand. In acting, man creates a new reality, new conditions, by that action."[36]

At issue here is the very nature of freedom. During the Dubček era, freedom was one of the basic philosophical issues under discussion. According to Lochman, the Czechs employed the young Marx in disputing the received opinion that freedom is the recognition of necessity. Said Lochman: "Freedom respects reality, but, at the same time, it stresses that reality is not just a set of conditions as they are given. Epistemologically, this means that there are no omniscient groups of people who can simply define what reality is. Reality is a creative process for which people are responsible."[37] Obviously, the attack on determinism was also an attack on the legitimacy of an omniscient, "voluntarist" Party. Curiously, one of those who inspired this focus on the young Marx in Czechoslovakia was Roger Garaudy.[38]

According to Peter Ludz, revisionism "provided the philosophical and ideological background of the mass revolutionary mood that emerged in Czechoslovakia during 1968."[39] This revisionism was based on the concept of man as a free individual who is free to choose his own ideology and conduct his life creatively and critically, without interference from the Party. It was also based on a renunciation of the elite and vanguard role of the Party in favor of popular participation in the political process.

Naturally, the revisionists radically revised the key concept of *partiinost* or "Party-mindedness." They took the concept back to its distant roots in the young Marx; they resurrected the young Marx's concept of *praxis,* according to which the individual is free to create his own history. As Ludz said, this latter view opened the door to dialogue with Christians and is the ideological precondition for political pluralism. The revisionists did not merely want "democratization" of the establishment, they wanted democracy as the word is understood in the West.[40] According to Victor A. Velen, the Czechoslovak combination of democracy and socialism was a return to the pre-Marxian utopian socialism and anarchism of Saint-Simon, Fourier, Proudhon, and Kropotkin.[41]

Writing prior to the Soviet invasion, Ross Terrill noted that real democracy depended on whether the vanguard role of the Party could be overcome. Terrill astutely assessed the situation when he reported: "Dubcek [sic] still speaks as if the New Course is a party affair. Yet it has gone beyond the party, in theory as in practice."[42] Non-Communist political activity was springing up everywhere. The old phantom parties of the National Front, the People's and National Socialist parties, were taking on new life. (The latter party was not a Nazi party.) The shackles had been taken off the media and the churches. There was talk of splitting the Communist Party in two as well as reviving the old Social Democratic Party (which had been coercively amalgamated into the Communist Party when the Communists took over in 1948).

Although the Communist Party had confirmed its intention to surrender its "monopolistic concentration of power," it did not want the possibility of losing governmental authority to an opposition party. The Party was in the precarious position of granting freedom of expression to opposition elements but forbidding them the chance to form a government. It was by no means clear that the Party could contain the swelling tide of opposition within acceptable limits. Although the Party encouraged the revival of the other parties in the National Front, it was adamantly against an opposition party outside the Front, as well as a resuscitation of the Social Democratic Party. However, because of freedom of expression, the Communist Party's stand was openly challenged by non-Communists as well as liberal Party members. Edward Taborsky summarized the situation well: "With the party sharply criticized in the mass media, its 'moral and political right' to leadership questioned, independent noncommunist groups springing into action and open arguments advanced for opposition parties, the Soviet leaders might have concluded that the 'counter-revolutionary forces' were indeed succeeding in their attempts to 'abolish the party's leading role.' "[43]

Of the many reforms that were to be institutionalized at the September 1968 Party Congress (which never took place because of the invasion), four were basic: (1) Competing candidates for Party office were to be elected by secret ballot of the rank and file. (2) The formation of factions within the Party was to be legalized—that is, the cornerstone of the democratic centralist organization of the Party (the proscription of factionalism) was to be forsaken. This had, however, already been accomplished de facto. (3) Autonomous social organizations, free from Party control (youth and trade unions, for example) were to be legalized. These reforms had also been realized de facto. (4) Freedom of speech and the press was to be guaranteed. This too existed de facto.[44]

Two things are significant about these reforms. First, in almost every case the Party was put in the feeble position of ratifying reforms that already existed in fact. The Party was not in control of the situation. The Party was not functioning as a Leninist Party; it was following or (in Leninist terminology) "tailing" the masses, not leading them. Second, even if the Party could have contained the situation, with the legalization of the above reforms it was clear that the Party would lose its grip on society. It would even lose its grip on itself. With the democratization of the Party and the legitimization of factions, today's minority could become tomorrow's majority. That is, today the Party might insist on its "leadership," but tomorrow it might change its stance. Anything could happen were the leadership of the Party to be in principle always up for grabs. A democratic Party would find it very difficult to protect itself from "irresponsible" and counterrevolutionary elements. The leaders of such a Party would have a hard time enforcing discipline and doctrinal orthodoxy. In short, the Party would lose the unity of action so vital to any Leninist party.

With the monopolistic role and monolithic character of the Party gone and the leading role of the Party in question, socialism itself hung in the balance—so far as the Soviets were concerned. The Soviets were able to point out that no country has sustained a fully socialist society without a monopolistic, monolithic, and vanguard Marxist-Leninist party. (Although they were not able to point to it then, Chile is the latest case in point.) Moreover, Czechoslovakia's political, economic, and military orientation to the Soviet Union was uncertain. Furthermore, the example of Czechoslovakia could have been contagious. Wrote Hans J. Morgenthau: "The Czechoslovak reforms conjured up the specter of slow erosion which . . . could spread throughout the Communist world, destroying the monopoly of political power of the Soviet Communist Party itself."[45] It is no wonder, then, that the Soviets decided to invade Czechoslovakia. Nor is it any wonder that they manifest a mortal fear of revisionism in general.

NOTES

1. Leopold Labedz, "Introduction," *Revisionism,* Labedz, ed. (New York: Praeger, 1962), p. 23.
2. A. James Gregor, *A Survey of Marxism* (New York: Random House, 1965), p. 132. Italics added.

3. Helmut Gollwitzer, *The Christian Faith and the Marxist Criticism of Religion* (New York: Scribner's, 1970), p. 2

4. Alasdair MacIntyre, *Marxism and Christianity,* rev. ed. (New York: Schocken, 1968), p. 113. Raymond Aron has noted that such interpretations are "commonplace" [R. Aron, *The Opium of the Intellectuals* (New York: Norton, 1962), p. 265].

5. William Hordern, *Christianity, Communism and History* (New York: Abingdon, 1954), p. 59.

6. See Karl Marx, "Contribution to the Critique of Hegel's Philosophy of Right," *Early Writings,* T. B. Bottomore, ed. (New York: McGraw–Hill, 1964), p. 52.

7. Karl Marx, "Foreword to Thesis: *The Difference Between the Natural Philosophy of Democritus and the Natural Philosophy of Epicurus,*" *On Religion,* Karl Marx and Friedrich Engels (New York: Schocken, 1964), p. 15.

8. Eric Voegelin, *The New Science of Politics* (Chicago: University of Chicago Press, 1952), p. 125.

9. See Robert C. Tucker, *Philosophy and Myth in Karl Marx* (London: Cambridge University Press, 1961), pp. 99–100.

10. Karl Marx, "Economic and Philosophical Manuscripts," *Early Writings,* T. B. Bottomore, ed., p. 165.

11. Karl Marx, "Foreword to Thesis . . . ," *On Religion,* Karl Marx and Friedrich Engels, p. 15n.

12. Manuel Azcárate, "Exceptional Spain," *Dialogue* (Vienna), *I* (Spring 1968), p. 102.

13. Marx, "Contribution to the Critque of Hegel's Philosophy of Right," *On Religion,* p. 41.

14. *Ibid.,* p. 42.

15. *Ibid.*

16. Portugal is perhaps the exception. For details on current relations between Marxists and Catholics in France and Italy, see Dale Vree, "Coalition Politics on the Left in France and Italy," *The Review of Politics, 37* (July 1975), pp. 340–356.

17. Louis Dupré, "Marx and Religion: An Impossible Marriage," *New Theology No. 6,* Martin E. Marty and Dean G. Peerman, eds. (New York: Macmillan, 1969), p. 153. In the words of a leading East German Marxist student of religion, "The analysis of religion by Marx and Engels differs from all the previous ones in that the question

of the truth or falseness of religious dogmas is not the focal point. . . . " [Olof Klohr, "Theoretische Grundsaetze und Aufgaben der Soziologie der Religion," *Religion und Atheismus Heute,* Klohr, ed. (East Berlin: Deutscher Verlag der Wissenschaften, 1966), p. 13] (the translation is mine). On the necessity of atheism to Marx's thought, see Peter M. Schuller, "Karl Marx's Atheism," *Science and Society, XXXIX* (Fall 1975), pp. 331–345, and Richard Lichtman, "The Marxian Critique of Christianity," *Marxism and Christianity,* Herbert Aptheker, ed. (New York: Humanities Press, 1968), pp. 65–121.

18. Helmut Gollwitzer, *The Demands of Freedom* (New York: Harper & Row, 1965), p. 138.

19. *Ibid.,* pp. 138–139.

20. Erich Fromm, *Marx's Concept of Man* (New York: Ungar, 1961), pp. 5, 64.

21. It is difficult to believe that Marx's major writings on alienation— "The Economic and Philosophical Manuscripts" and *Grundrisse*— are a central and indispensable part of Marxism properly so-called, inasmuch as Marx and Engels never tried to publish them, and indeed regarded them as a source of some embarrassment. See Lewis S. Feuer, "What Is Alienation? The Career of a Concept," *Marx and the Intellectuals* (Garden City, N.Y.: Anchor, 1969), pp. 81–85; Daniel Bell, "The Debate on Alienation," *Revisionism,* Labedz, ed., pp. 205–211; and J. E. Seigel, "Big Problem for Marx," review of *Karl Marx: His Life and Thought* by David McLellan, and *Grundrisse* by Karl Marx, *The New York Review of Books, XXI* (October 31, 1974), p. 35.

22. Louis Althusser, *For Marx* (New York: Vintage, 1969), pp. 10, 11–13. It should be noted that Althusser—and particularly some of his followers—have been charged with harboring Maoist sympathies. Nevertheless, Althusser has retained his status as one of the leading intellectuals in the French Communist Party. For a juxtaposition of the Soviet view (represented by E. M. Sitnikov) and a revisionist view (represented by Iring Fetscher), see "Soviet Society and the Problem of Alienation," *Marx and Marxism,* Iring Fetscher (New York: Herder and Herder, 1971), pp. 312–354.

23. Michael Harrington, "Marx versus Marx," *New Politics, 1* (Fall 1961), p. 114.

24. Gregor, *op. cit.,* pp. 164, 167.
25. "Engels to J. Bloch," Karl Marx and Frederick Engels, *Selected Works in Two Volumes* (Moscow: Foreign Languages Publishing House, 1962), II: p. 488.
26. Karl Marx, "Theses on Feuerbach," *Marx and Engels: Basic Writings on Politics and Philosophy,* Lewis S. Feuer, ed. (Garden City, N.Y.: Anchor, 1959), p. 244.
27. Marx, "The Eighteenth Brumaire of Louis Bonaparte," *Selected Works in Two Volumes,* I: p. 247.
28. "Engels to J. Bloch," *loc. cit.*
29. See V. I. Lenin, *What Is to Be Done?* (New York: International, 1969); Lenin, *Imperialism: The Highest Stage of Capitalism* (New York: International, 1969); Charles Taylor, "The Ambiguities of Marxist Doctrine," *The Student World, LI* (Second Quarter 1958), pp. 157–166; Y. A. Krasin, "Historical Necessity and Revolutionary Initiative," *Reprints from the Soviet Press* (New York), *XI* (October 2, 1970), pp. 14–31; Alfred G. Meyer, *Leninism* (New York: Praeger, 1957); Robert C. Tucker, "Stalinism and 'Transformism,' " *Stalin,* T. H. Rigby, ed. (Englewood Cliffs, N.J.: Prentice-Hall, 1966), pp. 60–64; Reinhold Niebuhr, *The Irony of American History* (New York: Scribner's, 1962), p. 80; and Andrew C. Janos, "The Communist Theory of the State and Revolution," *Communism and Revolution,* Cyril E. Black and Thomas P. Thornton, eds. (Princeton: Princeton University Press, 1964), pp. 27–41. The special cognitive and seemingly superhuman power that Marxist-Leninists attribute to the Party was superbly captured in one of Bertolt Brecht's poems, "Lob der Partei," from *Gedichte* (Frankfurt a. M.: Suhrkamp, 1961), III: p. 68.
30. Richard T. DeGeorge, *The New Marxism* (New York: Pegasus, 1968), pp. 68, 69, 67. Also see P. Yudin, *From Socialism to Communism* (Moscow: Progress Publishers, n.d.).
31. DeGeorge, *Soviet Ethics and Morality* (Ann Arbor: University of Michigan Press, 1969), pp. 115–116.
32. Fromm, *op. cit.,* p. 60.
33. Mihailo Markovíc, "Humanism and Dialectic," *Socialist Humanism,* Erich Fromm, ed. (Garden City, N.Y.: Anchor, 1965), pp. 96, 95.
34. Bronislaw Baczko, "Marx and the Idea of the Universality of Man," *Socialist Humanism,* Erich Fromm, ed., p. 196.

35. Danilo Pejović, "On the Power and Impotence of Philosophy," *Socialist Humanism,* Erich Fromm, ed., pp. 208–209. Roger Garaudy echoes similar sentiments: "Not only socialism, the first step of communism, but communism itself will not put an end to every kind of alienation" [R. Garaudy, *Reconquête de l'espoir* (Paris: Grasset, 1971), p. 132 (the translation is mine).]

36. Jan M. Lochman, "Marxism, Liberalism, and Religion: An East European Perspective," *Marxism and Radical Religion,* John C. Raines and Thomas Dean, eds. (Philadelphia: Temple University Press, 1970), p. 17.

37. *Ibid.,* p. 18.

38. See Vladimir V. Kusin, *The Intellectual Origins of the Prague Spring* (London: Cambridge University Press, 1971), p. 45.

39. Peter Ludz, "The 'New Socialism': Philosophy in Search of Reality," *Problems of Communism, XVIII* (July-October 1969), p. 33.

40. See *ibid.,* pp. 34–39.

41. See Victor A. Velen, "Why Moscow Fears the Czechs," *The New Leader, LI* (August 26, 1968), pp. 5–6.

42. Ross Terrill, "Czechoslovakia's New Course: Will Liberalization Lead to Democratization?" *The New Republic, 158* (May 18, 1968), p. 23. Also see Kusin, *op. cit.,* p. 140n.

43. Edward Taborsky, "The New Era in Czechoslovakia," *East Europe, 17* (November 1968), p. 26. This was indeed the basic thrust of the Soviet point of view (exaggeration notwithstanding). See Editorial, "Defense of Socialism is the Highest Internationalist Duty," *Pravda,* August 22, 1968, pp. 2–3. The complete text is translated into English in *The Current Digest of the Soviet Press, XX* (September 11, 1968), pp. 5–14. It is characteristic of revisionists of all countries to reject the Leninist concept of the leading role of the Party. See Wolfgang Leonhard, *Three Faces of Marxism* (New York: Holt, Rinehart and Winston, 1974), p. 309.

44. See Taborsky, *op cit.,* pp. 19–28.

45. Hans J. Morgenthau, "The Fate of Czechoslovakia: Why the Soviet Union Moved In," *The New Republic, 159* (December 7, 1968), p. 20. "The final decision to intervene was made . . . because the Soviets and their allies feared that the Czechoslovak defection from Communist orthodoxy would imperil the solidarity of the [Soviet bloc] alliance and spread heresy to their own lands. They

saw the experiment of the Czechs and Slovaks . . . as an infection
that could undermine their conception of what a communist state
should be. They believed it would weaken the communist party's
control over the state apparatus and unleash an uncontrollable
range of opinion. In a sense they were right" [Ronald Steel, "Up
Against the Wall in Prague," *The New York Review of Books, XI*
(September 26, 1968), p. 14].

5

Dialogical Marxism:
Roger Garaudy

> The theoretical and practical efforts of the revisionists
> are in the final analysis always subordinated to their
> attempt to liquidate the Party or to transform it into
> a reformist organization.
>
> FUNDAMENTALS OF MARXISM-LENINISM: MANUAL
> (Moscow, 1963)

CONTRADICTION AND RESOLUTION

Both Marxists and Christians have accused one another of denying man his freedom and initiative. Consequently, human freedom and initiative have become imperatives around which the
dialogue revolves. For example, speaking for dialogical Marxists,
Garaudy has said: "The objection that keeps coming up for us

151

always appears when it seems that Christianity is taking away from man the initiative he should have in history, either by reason of a teleological or a dogmatic conception of Providence or by reason of the conception of original sin. . . ."[1] It has been shown how far Cox and Moltmann have gone to meet this objection, and how far as a consequence they have traveled from normative Christianity. Of interest to us here is the way in which Garaudy has sought to measure up to his own standards for human initiative and freedom, and the distance he has traveled from normative Marxism in so doing.

Garaudy began his career in the Party as a loyal Stalinist. When Khrushchev startled the Communist world by denouncing Stalin, and the Kremlin ordered de-Stalinization, Garaudy dutifully jettisoned his Stalinism and changed his line. Perhaps he learned his lesson too well. De-Stalinization had a profound effect on Garaudy, and he became impatient with the slow, halting, and irregular pace of de-Stalinization since 1956. Garaudy's alienation from the French Party began in 1966 with his heavy involvement in the Marxist-Christian dialogue and reached a crisis point when the French Party for all intents and purposes ratified the Soviet invasion of Czechoslovakia. At that point Garaudy's divorce from the Party became a foregone conclusion. In 1970 he was finally expelled.[2] Currently he is Professor of Philosophy and Aesthetics at the University of Poitiers. In what follows I shall analyze Garaudy's thought as it relates to dialogue with Christians—beginning with a scrutiny of his preexpulsion thought.

Garaudy's persistent emphasis on human freedom and initiative is evidence of his attraction to the young Marx (although he has been reluctant to admit this attraction in print, perhaps for fear of revealing to his Party comrades his real source of inspiration). It is a long and difficult road to traverse from Stalin back to the young Marx, especially when one tries to follow the Party line along the way. In reacting strongly against philosophical Stalinism, he has nevertheless professed his fidelity to Leninism—perhaps to safeguard his Party credentials, perhaps out of a habitual loyalty to Lenin, or perhaps simply out of conviction. Whatever the case, this is an impossible position to maintain since the philosophical differences between Stalin and Lenin are minimal (regardless of their differences as political leaders). Likewise, in championing the values of the young Marx he has affirmed his Leninism. This too is an impossible position since the philosophical differences between Lenin and the young Marx are fundamental. In short, Garaudy has attempted to divorce Stalin from Lenin in order to marry Lenin to the young Marx. The result has been confusion and contradiction.

Garaudy's problem stems from the strong emphasis on human freedom, creativity, and disalienation that is explicit in the dialogue. He recognizes that the affirmation of human liberty is the basis of Marx's atheism. In this spirit, he passionately seeks to affirm man's ontological freedom, that man alone is the creator of his history and destiny, and that man is not the alienated servant of either God, history, or Party. Yet, he is aware that Marxism speaks the language of lawful historical necessity, and that such necessity often bears resemblance to a kind of "divine Providence." Hence, Marxism seems to free man from servitude to God, only to subject him to the objective forces of history and the impersonal imperatives of class and/or Party. Garaudy is dimly aware of this dilemma and has great difficulty in fighting his way free of it.

For example, he has said of the Party: "It is oriented to a consciousness of the *objective laws of historical development* which delineate the perspectives of the working class and enable it to discover scientifically, by the analysis of objective conditions, the means to victory." Lest there should be any doubt about the matter, he added that the Party has "superior advantages of cognition."[3] This is pure Leninism (as well as pure Stalinism). However, elsewhere Garaudy throws out the Party's superior cognition. He denounces the "myth of absolute truth" because "murderous and authoritarian methods are the inevitable fruit of the necessity to impose that truth from above."[4] He seems to be oblivious of the fact that Lenin regarded truth (and the truth of Marxism) as objective and absolute,[5] and that Lenin can be understood to have instituted "murderous and authoritarian methods."

It is impossible to imagine that Garaudy can at one and the same time affirm the "objective laws" of history and still deny those laws the status of "absolute truth." Can objective laws be only relatively true? If this is possible, Garaudy does not explain how. If he means that the truth of Marxism is only relative, then he would be better off speaking of "tendencies" and "probabilities" rather than objective laws (although this would not in itself solve the problem of human freedom). If, on the other hand, he were to insist that Marxism has uncovered the objective laws of history and that the Party has superior cognition in perceiving those laws, then it is inconceivable that the truth of Marxism-Leninism could be anything other than objective and absolute. Then, since freedom is the recognition of necessity, and since the Party has a monopoly on perception of historical necessity, freedom would consist of obeying the will of the Party (hence, we get *partiinost*—which is functionally equivalent to the "freedom" Christians claim for themselves in obeying the will of Christ).

Garaudy does not seem to be aware of the contradiction in which he has involved himself. He is even able to contain that contradiction in a single sentence, to wit: "Man is *totally responsible* for becoming not what he is but what he is not yet and what is nowhere set down; and at the same time he is obliged to be conscious of the historical conditions created by man's earlier creations which obey *necessary laws,* to neglect or make light of which leads to fortuity and impotence."[6] What we have here is another version of that *studied ambiguity* we met in the thought of Cox and Moltmann. That man is totally responsible for his future (hence totally free) and yet obliged to conform to history's necessary laws is certainly mysterious. But Garaudy prefers to delight in this mystery rather than give it rational explanation, for he says that man's creation of his own history is "at the same time and indivisibly necessary and free."[7] Walter Odajnyk has summarized the terms of the problem, which is a problem of Marxism in general: "It is quite safe for Marxism to state that man makes his own history, for who else is there to make it; it is a tautology. But once certain restrictions are placed upon man's freedom in creating his own history . . . then man is still making his own history, yet certainly not as a free being."[8]

Hence, when Garaudy says (in a book primarily addressed to Christians) that Marx's economic determinism is merely a supposition and contrary to "the basic spirit of his doctrine" which is "essentially a method of historical initiative,"[9] one gets the impression that he is setting up straw men, and has either deluded himself or attempted to delude his audience with empty rhetoric. He tends to use the term "economic determinism" as a synonym for "mechanistic materialism," a moribund form of materialism within the Marxist ambit, having been disavowed by Marx, Engels, Lenin, and Stalin alike. Likewise, his understanding of "historical initiative" does not seem to differ markedly from the understanding of the concept by Marx, Engels, Lenin, or Stalin. Thus, while Garaudy is inspired by the jargon of neo-Marxism, the substance of what he says does not seem to deviate at this point from standard Marxism.

However, sometimes Garaudy transcends the level of confusion and contradiction, and seems to be serious about his neo-Marxist rhetoric. Not only does he denounce absolute truth, but he asserts that Communists "do not have an exclusive hold on the truth,"[10] thus crippling the notion of the Party's superior cognition. Furthermore, he claims that the truth of Marxism is methodological, not "dogmatic." Marxism is a critical and experimental method that fosters continual growth in knowledge; it is not an absolute truth in the sense of being a dogma immune from and superior to scientific and social scientific discoveries. It is not a "metaphysical" materialism depriving man of his freedom and initiative.

"To be faithful to Marx," Garaudy has said, "means to be faithful not to the texts, as if these were sacred texts, but to use his method, which is a method of always going beyond."[11] By the Marxian method he means looking at historical events as multicausal, although ultimately caused by social factors.[12] But such a method (when isolated from the substantive tenets of the Marxian texts) is not unlike that of Western social science. To be committed to a "method of always going beyond" is nothing more than being committed to the principles of testing (verification or falsification) in ordinary science. Garaudy's "Marxism" advances neither absolute truth, objective laws, nor substantive doctrines. One is left wondering what is peculiarly "Marxist" about this since, by Garaudy's standards, there could no more be a Marxist social science than there could be a Marxist chemistry. According to Maurice Cranston, a Marxism of this sort would

cease to be an ideology and . . . would cease to provide clear theoretical guidelines for the general public—indeed, it would cease to a large extent to offer any clear-cut answers to the more important questions that it raises. It would simply summon people to further inquiry. . . .

Hence . . . Marxism . . . would no longer be of use to any
authoritarian regime. . . . It could not possibly serve as a "state
philosophy."[13]

Cranston therefore appropriately concluded that the French
Party's condemnation of Garaudy made good sense from a Party
point of view.

Hence, at this point, in pursuing indeterminacy and a non-
dogmatic, "non-Providential" Marxism, Garaudy has placed
himself outside the tradition of Marxism-Leninism, which is not
only more than a methodology, but depends on its superior
cognitive powers for its authority and legitimacy. From
Garaudy's perspective it is clear that the Party can have no cognitive function. Those seeking empirical truth would be better
advised to look to the universities. Furthermore, in a socialist
society, the Party can have no legitimate claim to a monopoly of
power or a vanguard role because it has no legitimate claim to
a privileged hold on truth. It is understandable, then, why Garaudy had such a sympathy for the developments in Dubček's
Czechoslovakia.

In summary, Garaudy seems at this point to represent a figure
in transition. On the one hand, he affirms the libertarian values
of the young Marx while maintaining a verbal allegiance to the
lawful necessitarianism and claims to superior cognition of
Marxism-Leninism. The result is confusion and contradiction.
On the other hand, he tends to resolve this contradiction by
opting for the libertarian values, rejecting the above claims to
superior cognition, and interpreting the above necessitarianism
in terms of tendencies and corrigible hypotheses of a general
social science. The basic trend of his thought is in the direction
of the latter resolution. As such, Garaudy's Marxism collapses.

It is clear that the obsession of dialogue-makers with full human freedom and initiative and an open and undetermined fu-

ture is fundamentally subversive of orthodox Marxism (as it is of orthodox Christianity).

THE QUESTION OF PERSECUTION

One of Garaudy's primary objectives in the dialogue is to convince Christians that were his type of Marxist to come to power in France and elsewhere, Christians would have no need to fear persecution. He proceeds to make some major concessions; however, he always leaves open a loophole, arousing the suspicion that his argument is either inconsistent, misinformed, or disingenuous.

For example, he said: "The arrival of socialism should not lead to atheism becoming the state religion. . . . Certainly in a Communist society, the Party can, and should, struggle against religious ideology . . . with theoretical criticism. But what applies to the Party does not apply to the State."[14] This position appears to be a big step in the direction of a truly laicist state and ideological coexistence (at least so far as religion and atheism are concerned). However, Garaudy claims his position is akin to Lenin's—which it is! Lenin said: "We demand that religion be held a private affair so far as the state is concerned. But by no means can we consider religion a private affair so far as our Party is concerned." And: "to us the ideological struggle is not a private affair, but the affair of the whole Party, of the whole proletariat."[15] Like Garaudy, Lenin says that the Party, not the state, is to promote atheism. This too sounds like a promise of a laicist state and ideological coexistence. But when the Party equates itself with the proletariat and when, under socialism, the proletariat is the only class and represents all of society, the distinction between state and Party is spurious. Not surprisingly, Lenin's "promise" was not kept. What reason is there to believe that Garaudy's "promise" will be kept? Such guarantees mean nothing when the functions of the state are subordinate to, and overlap, the functions of the Party. It would seem that the only secure guarantee of a laicist state would be a multiparty system where the Communist Party can be voted out of office (because it does not claim to speak for the whole proletariat or the whole society) and where there is an independent judiciary able and willing to protect constitutional rights.

However, Garaudy appears to take another step toward accommodation. He has said that "it in no way follows from the principles of Marxism that in a socialist regime power should be exercised by one party alone, the Communist party." He seems to be holding up the possibility of a genuine coalition government in the Western sense. But, unfortunately, he points to Bulgaria, "where power is exercised conjointly by the Communist Party and the Peasant Party," as an example of what he has in mind.[16] It is astonishing that Garaudy does not know, or does not think his audience knows, that non-Communist parties in Eastern Europe (including Bulgaria) are nothing but appendages of the ruling Communist Party—nothing but "phantom parties," as East European area specialists often call them. What Garaudy appears to grant with his right hand, he takes away with his left.

Garaudy takes yet another approach. He argues in effect that persecution of religion under socialism is not necessary because religion is an epiphenomenon of alienated societies, and as such must gradually wither away under socialism as alienation is progressively overcome. He is aware that religion has survived in socialist societies longer than was originally expected. Curiously, he feels compelled to find an explanation for this survival in "objective conditions." Garaudy, along with neo-Marxists in general, contends that alienation still exists in socialist societies, and he finds in this alienation the "objective" explanation for the persistence of religion.[17] Logically, therefore, the way to do away with religion is not to persecute religion by administrative measures, but to attack the social and economic roots of religion—that is, the remaining sources of alienation. It is puzzling that Garaudy would take recourse in the economic determinism of which he had previously so handily disposed by pronouncing it erroneous to believe that when the economic and social conditions of socialism are realized "the superstructures necessarily derive from them, and that man is going to be transformed automatically. . . ."[18] He seems to have forgotten about his adamant renunciation of objective laws and materialist reductionism as well as his repeated insistence on the relative autonomy of the superstructure.

Soviet Marxists readily admit the relative autonomy of the superstructure *in a socialist society*. Hence, they find no need to locate the cause of the persistence of religion in the socialist substructure. They point instead to the lag of superstructural changes behind substructural changes, as well as to miscellaneous factors such as the cultural influence of the West and ineffective atheist propaganda. Furthermore, according to Leninism (and Stalinism) the active and creative element in mankind is found in the proletariat and, more particularly, in its conscious vanguard, the Communist Party. The conditioned element in mankind is found in the rest of humanity. Under socialism, the Party seizes control of the state and thereby of the superstructure of the society. The superstructure then can be, as Richard T. DeGeorge has put it, "an active—and even a motor— influence in the development of socialist society."[19] Therefore, a Communist Party can come to power in an underdeveloped and precapitalist society and create a socialist culture and economy by administrative means. There is no need to wait for "objective conditions" to take their own course. Hence, Lenin's "voluntarism" (which Garaudy praises profusely) can lead directly to those "murderous and authoritarian methods" (which he roundly denounces). Therefore, if in a socialist society religion endures (for superstructural reasons), it is entirely appropriate for the state to take police and administrative (superstructural) measures against religion.

One might ask, why should the state attack religion? It is frequently pointed out that the "totalitarian" character of the Communist state cannot tolerate any rival ideology or independent institution. Furthermore, the Leninist view of religion stipulates that in modern times religion is invariably an opiate, dissipating the will of the workers to struggle and achieve full communism. There is, however, a more profound reason. It has to do with the nature of communism in its final and perfected form. Under communism there will be no state, no police, and no legal machinery. The will to conform to social norms will be spontaneous and internal, rather than (largely) coerced and external as in precommunist society. However, under communism there is no room for (and no need for) disagreement over morality, customs, philosophy, economics, and so forth. All of these fundamental issues must be settled in advance. Everyone must willfully subscribe to the official Marxist-Leninist view on these matters if there is to be a harmonious and self-regulating society. Dissident ideologies and religions would inevitably inspire dissident attitudes and behavior, hence destroying the comprehensive uniformity prerequisite to the perfected society. Dissidence leads to factionalism, which leads to conflict, which leads to politics, which then requires courts, laws, police, and all the paraphernalia of political power.

Full communism is not just a "better" society, it is the "best," the ultimate, the perfect society; it is a messianic fulfillment for which every honest Marxist-Leninist must strive and sacrifice. To tolerate rival ideologies and religions (for other than tactical reasons) is to stall and frustrate the redemption of humanity. The Soviet Union does not take a laissez-faire attitude toward such "survivals of capitalism" as crime, parasitism, money-grubbing, hooliganism, careerism, racism, and drunkenness. Neither does it take a hands-off attitude toward religion. Nor—given its philosophical premises—should it. According to Marxist-Leninist theory, communist consciousness does not arise spontaneously or automatically. Hence, it must be inculcated by means of education, law, social pressure, and (where deemed necessary) draconian police methods. Thus, there can be no scruples against taking legal and extralegal measures against religion and religious people; in fact, such measures represent a moral imperative.

Therefore, whenever a Marxist such as Garaudy suggests that the persecution of religion is "un-Marxist," hence unnecessary, because religion is merely a reflex of "objective conditions" which remain to be transformed, he is either deluding himself or his Christian partners in dialogue. Whatever the case, he will certainly be giving his Marxist-Leninist peers cause for outrage.

However, even here Garaudy leaves himself a loophole. He denies that believers are persecuted in the Soviet Union. Whatever difficulties Christians have experienced are explained and excused under two rubrics: (1) The Orthodox Church was the handmaiden of Czarism and supported the couterrevolution, hence by implication it deserved the persecution it suffered. (2) Although there is no persecution today, there is some "bureaucratic vexation" on the local level.[20]

This is a patently misinformed and/or self-serving analysis of the situation. (1) If Garaudy were correct, then one would expect that only the Orthodox Church had suffered at the hands of the state. But we know that all religious groups, Orthodox and non-Orthodox, Christian and non-Christian, have been persecuted. Curiously, today the Orthodox Church is one of the least persecuted religious groups; the degree of historical corruption in a religious group had very little to do with how that group was treated. Lenin regarded a progressive and pure religion to be far more dangerous than a corrupt religion. After denouncing "all religious ideas" as an "unspeakable abomination," he went on to say:

> The crowd is much more able to see through millions of *physical* sins, dirty tricks, violences and infections which are therefore much less dangerous than is the *subtle,* spiritual idea of the little god arrayed in the smartest of "ideological" costumes. A Catholic priest who violates young girls is *much less* dangerous to [socialist] "democracy" than are priests who do not wear surplices, priests without vulgar religion, ideological and democratic priests, who preach the creation and making of little gods. The first type of priest can be *easily* exposed, condemned, and driven out—but the second *cannot* be driven out so simply. It is a thousand times more difficult to expose *him.* . . . [21]

(2) To suggest that there is no systematic effort emanating from Moscow to liquidate coercively all religion is to contradict virtually all the responsible scholarship that has been done on the subject.[22] It is one thing for Garaudy to declare that persecution is an inappropriate way for socialist societies to deal with religion. But when he proceeds to deny the existence of persecution in the USSR and makes bogus excuses for the difficulties Christians have experienced there, the Christian winds up where he started, having gained nothing. Again, what Garaudy seems to grant with his right hand, he takes away with his left.

Adding insult to injury (so far as the Christian is concerned), Garaudy says that the obvious objection to Marxist-Christian dialogue, namely, that Communists preach tolerance when out of power but practice persecution when in power, is "both wrong-headed and improper" and *"intégriste* in origin."[23] What is really improper is to suppose that the integralist (right-wing) Catholics have a monopoly on this objection. For instance, at least two prominent progressive Catholics (Karl Rahner, S.J. and Quentin Lauer, S.J.) have raised precisely this issue.[24] Garaudy's glib handling of this weighty objection is most puzzling.

In sum, on the issue of the treatment of Christians in a socialist society, Garaudy's performance is alternately deceptive, misinformed, or self-contradictory. It is difficult to see how hardthinking Christians could find satisfaction with Garaudy at this point.

GARAUDY EXCOMMUNICATED

So far, the direction of Garaudy's thought has been revisionist; however, the precise formulation of his ideas has frequently been hesitant, ambiguous, and contradictory, perhaps out of deference to the Party and to protect his position in the Party.

However, because of the Soviet invasion of Czechoslovakia, Garaudy probably felt he could no longer hide his true feelings and inclinations behind ambiguities. His position within the French Party and the pro-Soviet camp became untenable. He had completely identified his own understanding of socialism with the Czechoslovak Spring. When the USSR crushed socialism "with a human face" and the French Party quickly reconciled itself to the Soviet actions, Garaudy probably could no longer contain himself. The result was a major work, *The Crisis in Communism* (published in France in 1969 as *Le Grand tournant du socialisme*). Although he still claims to be a true Marxist and a true Leninist, this book represents what can plausibly be taken to be a frank statement of his views. Many of the previously cited ambiguities are resolved in a clearly heretical manner. It is possible that he wrote the book knowing full well that his days in the Party were numbered and hence felt free of the need to reconcile his views with the Party line. The book marks a new stage in Garaudy's thought. It is not surprising that the book constituted one of the justifications for his expulsion from the Party. As such, it is worth examining in some detail.

To begin with, Garaudy continues to talk in terms of objective laws of development, inevitability, and historical necessity.

However, these locutions are hyperbolic, for he clearly acknowledges that all economic, sociological, and historical "laws" merely express a tendency.[25] Although the force of a tendency is nowhere defined, he would seem to be trying to allow greater latitude for human freedom (although he does not speak of absolute freedom).

Garaudy further develops his theme that Marxism is a method, not a dogma with substantive content. He acknowledges that "Marx had revealed in *Capital* the general laws of the development of capitalism. . . ."[26] However, said Garaudy, these laws lost their validity in the early 1930s when capitalism changed its nature by adopting Keynesian techniques. Hence, Garaudy reduces Marxism to a method "that permits one, by analysing *present* contradictions, to foresee and realize the future possibilities."[27] The contradictions and possibilities that Marx analyzed no longer obtain. Having dispensed with the letter of Marxism, Garaudy proceeds, in a Marxian "spirit," to uncover new contradictions and possibilities in both capitalism and socialism. Hence, whether he frames these new discoveries in terms of laws or tendencies would seem to be irrelevant to doctrinal Marxism since these are not Marx's laws (or tendencies), but Garaudy's. To be sure, orthodox Marxism allows for new discoveries; however, the vital point here is that Garaudy's "development of doctrine" lacks any claim to authority since it comes from the pen of one man, not from the collective mind of the Party.

Garaudy frames his new discoveries in terms of tendencies, not laws. These tendencies are a product of the postindustrial revolution or "mutation" which, he says, is as momentous as the Industrial Revolution. There is no apparent reason why one must be a "Marxist" to analyze the postindustrial revolution and chart out the possibilities it offers for liberation from labor and alienation (especially since Marxism was a product of the industrial age, which has been superseded). Elsewhere, there is evidence that Garaudy has even lost Marxism's fundamental commitment to the manual worker, and to the class struggle (as *the* struggle of our time). In profoundly unMarxist fashion, he has declared that "no revolt has ever been founded on deeper grounds than that of contemporary youth."[28] More generally, because what characterizes postindustrial society is the vital role played by nonmanual or intellectual labor (where, noted Garaudy, "the essential productive force is less land or machines than knowledge"[29]), Garaudy tends to assign an importance to technicians, scientists, students, and other intellectuals that overshadows the primary importance traditionally assigned manual workers by the French Communist Party. (The terms of Garaudy's debate with the Party here are curiously analogous to the continuing debate within America's Democratic Party between members of its trade-union and "New Politics" wings.)

It becomes clear that the Party does not have superior powers of cognition and cannot lay claim to an exclusive hold on, or privileged insight into, truth. He rejects the idea that the Party is "omniscient and infallible," saying that such a view of the Party will "in the long run inevitably lead to bureaucratic, dogmatic and authoritarian distortion, to the degeneration of socialism."[30]

Garaudy further develops his heterodox views about the Party. Because he systematically denies the Leninist notion that the Party is privy to esoteric knowledge, the role of the Party undergoes drastic alteration. The Party can no longer lay claim to a monopoly of power and authority, nor can it play a vanguard role. Hence, it is obvious why Garaudy was so strongly sympathetic to the Czechoslovak experiment. It was because, among other things, prior to the Soviet invasion, the Party had ceded its monopoly role and was on the brink of losing its vanguard role.

Garaudy has become something of a participatory democrat.

Accordingly, the source of historical and political initiative does not rest with the Party, but with the people (who, under socialism, are to participate in decision-making through democratic institutions of self-management). The Party is merely to be a synthesizer, coordinator, and stimulator of the people's initiative. The Party does not even have a patent on this meager function. Rather, the Party must continually earn and give practical proof of its right to perform this function. Garaudy calls for pluralism, by which he means that non-Communists should have initiative in the political process of building socialism. Mercifully, he does *not* cite Bulgaria as an example of what he means. The logic of his argument suggests that Christians and other non-Communists could look forward to an equal role with Communists.

As we have already seen, Garaudy promised Christians freedom from persecution by calling for a separation of the Party from the state. What looked like a guarantee of ideological coexistence and a truly laicist state was obscured by the fact that Lenin has "promised" similar things. These promises were rendered meaningless because Lenin made the Party the spokesman for the whole proletariat and subordinated the state to the Party. Now, however, Garaudy's promise is made credible because initiative is the possession of the people (as individuals as well as an aggregate), not the Party. The state is not subordinated to the Party, nor is the Party the exclusive and eternal voice of the people (or proletariat). He goes one step further. Previously he said that the Party should promote atheism and the state should remain neutral. Now the Party not only does not promote atheism but does not even hold atheism to be a part of its philosophy. In fact, the Party does not even have a philosophy. Not only is the state laicist, so is the Party! Said Garaudy: "the Party . . . cannot afford to have an 'official philosophy', nor can it be in principle either idealist, materialist, religious or atheist."[31] Philosophy and politics must be "distinct entities." In fact, a (progressive) Christian should be able to hold a leading position in the Party (which is not now the case, even in those few Communist parties that admit Christians to rank and file membership).

Although Garaudy does not take the opportunity to revise his myopic estimate of the situation of Christians in the USSR, his overall opinion of the Soviet system is anything but apologetic. He claims, like other neo-Marxists, that the Soviet workers are alienated by the "bureaucratic-military complex" that runs the USSR and that the system is "contrary to the very principles of socialism." If there is not a "profound democratic renewal that will restore the true face of socialism" in the Soviet Union, then the result will be "reactionary neo-Bonapartism and the dictatorship of the army."[32] That is tantamount to charging that the USSR is on the road to fascism. Regardless of the merits of the argument here, one would have to conclude that Garaudy's previous denial that Christians are persecuted in the USSR was probably more a matter of ignorance than a deliberate attempt at distortion.

He correctly identifies the central issue at hand ("the great turning-point of socialism," in his words) as one's understanding of the Party. In addition to stripping the Party of any official philosophy, he calls for a dismantling of democratic centralism as it is currently practiced. He wants the initiative for decisions to come from the rank and file as well as from the leadership. He wants minority opinions within the Party to be made known and calls for a free circulation of ideas within the Party. The differences between his version of the Party and the orthodox Leninist version is immense; however, there does not appear to be any significant difference between his version and the model supplied by Social Democracy. More importantly for the dialogue, there is no indication that the Party is to be charged with the duty of crafting a "new man" who, as a citizen of a stateless and perfected communist society, would be so conditioned as to be unable and unwilling to dissent in thought, word, or deed. There would appear to be no desire whatever to coerce people into ideological uniformity, for the Party does not even impose ideological uniformity on itself.

It would be beside the point to stress that Garaudy does not regard atheism as essential to Marxism, for he does not even regard normative Marxism as essential to his brand of "Marxism." It is nevertheless true that he is neither militantly atheistic nor messianic (suggesting once again a connection between militant atheism and messianism in the socialist movement). For all the eschatological excitement aroused by the Marxist-Christian dialogue, the socialism Garaudy offers us is not only nonviolent and gradualist, but motivationally flat and colorless. For example, after having spent almost thirty pages analyzing the situation in the United States, he winds up issuing a call, not for socialism, but for "a capitalism that has human goals," "a purposeful capitalism."[33]

Garaudy's *The Crisis in Communism* is a catalogue of heresies. Instead of rehearsing them all, suffice it to say that, all in all, there is no reason for Christians to fear persecution on account of their religion should Marxists of Garaudy's stripe ever succeed in coming to power. The price to be paid for this assurance is the abandonment of the Marxist-Leninist Party as well as the substance of the Marxist-Leninist ideology itself (the former seemingly being the guardian of the latter). Ironically, Christians have gained a sincere partner in dialogue, but it is highly doubtful that, in making dialogue with Garaudy, they will be making dialogue with a normative Marxist.

NOTES

1. *IH*, p. 4.
2. See Jean Daniel, "Les communistes après Garaudy," *Le Nouvel*

Observateur, No. 289 (May 25, 1970), pp. 20–22; "Roger Garaudy—Out with a Bang," *Le Monde Weekly,* May 27, 1970, p. 2; Alain Woodrow, "The Excommunication of Roger Garaudy," *Commonweal, XCII* (March 20, 1970), pp. 28–30; Roger Salloch, "The Dissent of Roger Garaudy," *The New Republic, 162* (March 7, 1970), pp. 17–19; Charles Andras, "The Christian-Marxist Dialogue," *East Europe, 17* (March 1968), p. 15; and Neil McInnes, "The Christian-Marxist Dialogue: International Implications," *Survey,* No. 67 (April 1968), p. 61. For the principal documents and speeches exchanged between Garaudy and his opponents in the Party, see Garaudy, *The Whole Truth* (London: Fontana/Collins, 1971), pp. 19–43, 45–83, 94–111, 116–120, 122–130, 134–160.

3. Roger Garaudy, *Karl Marx: The Evolution of His Thought* (New York: International, 1967), pp. 196, 197. Italics added.

4. *MTC,* p. 16.

5. See A. James Gregor, *A Survey of Marxism* (New York: Random House, 1965), p. 90, and Alfred G. Meyer, *Leninism* (New York: Praeger, 1957), p. 97.

6. *MTC,* p. 77. Italics added.

7. *Ibid.,* p. 78. In his study of Lenin, Garaudy wants to say that Lenin adhered—in "dialectical" fashion—to both the proposition that the Party enjoys superior consciousness and the proposition that the masses are equally privy to such consciousness by virtue of their legitimately "spontaneous initiative." But if the latter proposition is true, it is difficult to understand how the former one (which is a cornerstone of Soviet Marxism-Leninism) can be true at the same time. Garaudy's novel interpretation of Lenin clouds the issue at hand as well as casts into doubt the vanguard role of the Party. See R. Garaudy, *Lénine* (Paris: Presses Universitaries de France, 1968), p. 28.

8. Walter Odajnyk, *Marxism and Existentialism* (Garden City, N.Y.: Anchor, 1965), pp. 115–116.

9. *AD,* pp. 72–73.

10. *IH,* p. 18.

11. *Ibid.,* p. 13.

12. See *MTC,* pp. 56–57.

13. Maurice Cranston, "The Thought of Roger Garaudy," *Problems of Communism, XIX* (September-October 1970), p. 18.

14. Garaudy, "Creative Freedom," *The Christian Marxist Dialogue*, Paul Oestreicher, ed., (New York: Macmillan, 1969), p. 147.
15. V. I. Lenin, "Socialism and Religion" (pamphlet) (Moscow: Progress Publishers, 1968), pp. 4, 6.
16. Garaudy, *A Christian-Communist Dialogue* (Garden City, N.Y.: Doubleday, 1968), p. 177. Also see *IH*, p. 17.
17. See *MTC*, p. 123.
18. *Ibid.*, pp. 34–35.
19. Richard T. DeGeorge, *The New Marxism* (New York: Pegasus, 1968), p. 41.
20. See *AD*, pp. 65–66.
21. V. I. Lenin, *Religion* (New York: International, 1933), pp. 42–43.
22. See *inter alia* Walter Kolarz, *Religion in the Soviet Union* (London: Macmillan, 1961); Nikita Struve, *Christians in Contemporary Russia* (New York: Scribner's, 1967); Michael Bourdeaux, *Religious Ferment in Russia: Protestant Opposition to Soviet Religious Policy* (London: St. Martin's, 1968); Michael Bourdeaux, *Patriarch and Prophets: Persecution of the Russian Orthodox Church Today* (New York: Praeger, 1970); Richard H. Marshall, Jr., ed., *Aspects of Religion in the Soviet Union: 1917–67* (Chicago: University of Chicago Press, 1971); and the periodicals *Religion in Communist Dominated Areas* (New York) and *Religion in Communist Lands* (England).
23. *AD*, pp. 64–65.
24. See Edmund Demaitre, "The Christian-Marxist Dialogue," *Communist Affairs*, 5 (July-August 1967), p. 7, and Quentin Lauer, S.J., *A Christian-Communist Dialogue* (Garden City, N.Y.: Doubleday, 1968), p. 42.
25. *CC*, pp. 25, 50.
26. *Ibid.*, p. 77.
27. *Ibid.*, p. 51.
28. Garaudy, "New Goals for Socialism," *The Center Magazine*, V (September-October 1972), p. 33. Garaudy's differences with the French Party over the question of its relation to the student movement also played a role in his alienation from the Party. For information on these differences, see Garaudy, *Pour un modéle français du socialisme* (Paris: Gallimard, 1968), pp. 273–286; Garaudy, *The Whole Truth*, pp. 17–43; and Richard Johnson, *The French*

Communist Party versus the Students (New Haven: Yale University Press, 1972), pp. 101–110.

29. Garaudy, The Alternative Future: A Vision of Christian Marxism (New York: Simon and Schuster, 1974), p. 122.

30. CC, pp. 97, 107.

31. Ibid., p. 230.

32. Ibid., pp. 149, 139.

33. Ibid., pp. 249, 76. For the official response of the French Party's Politburo to this book, and Garaudy's rejoinder, see Garaudy, The Whole Truth, pp. 137–148. In his most recent major work, The Alternative Future, Garaudy carries forward the arguments he made in The Crisis in Communism (and other writings of the same period). He continues his assault on "dogmatic" Marxism and Leninist elitism. The major difference between the two books is that in The Crisis in Communism he deviated from Marxism-Leninism in a rightward, Social Democratic direction, whereas in his newer book he swings over to an "ultraleft" position, taking up the banner of anarcho-syndicalism. Furthermore, in contrast to his earlier judgments on Chinese Communism [see R. Garaudy, Le problème chinois (Paris: Seghers, 1967), pp. 7–242], he now praises the Chinese revolution for offering mankind the only desirable model for an alternative future. In The Alternative Future, Garaudy manifests a greater sympathy for Christianity than he has ever shown before. Although he has become neither an orthodox Christian nor even a theist, he is able to say: "It is an overwhelming experience when a man who has professed himself an atheist for many years discovers that there has always been a Christian inside him" (p. 177). For further comment on The Alternative Future, see Dale Vree, "Falling Out From the Dialogue," Worldview, 17 (December 1974), pp. 50–51. For a rather careful Soviet critique of Garaudy's thought, see H. Momjan, Marxism and the Renegade Garaudy (Moscow: Progress Publishers, 1974). It is significant that Momjan grudgingly admits that Garaudy's attempt to synthesize Marxism and Christianity is "unquestionably an important and considerable one" (even though "bound to end in failure"). Ibid., pp. 221, 180. Unfortunately, Garaudy's autobiography, Parole d'homme (Paris: Laffont, 1975) did not reach me in time to be discussed in this book.

Conclusion

I am afraid that this dialogue may end by glossing
over the real differences.
HERBERT MARCUSE

It has frequently been remarked that Communism is a secular religion, a Christian heresy, and the like. One often hears it said that Marx was subconsciously influenced by the Jewish prophets and by Christian symbolism and eschatology, and that Communism could only have been born and taken root in the Christian soil of Europe. Whatever the merits of these claims, it cannot be doubted that there is an affinity between Communism and heterodox Christian chiliasm. Several Marxist writers (including Engels), have noted this connection, to the point of declaring these chiliasts to be forerunners of socialism.

Nevertheless, the position of the Marxist movement has generally been that whereas before the discovery of scientific socialism, religion may have occasionally played a progressive

role, now that real (as opposed to illusory) human emancipation is in sight, religion can only play a reactionary role, even
when it pretends to be progressive. Marx and Engels said that
clerical socialism was actually a feudalistic phenomenon.
"Christian socialism," they declared, "is but the holy water with
which the priest consecrates the heartburnings of the
aristocrat."[1] According to Lenin, the dialectical materialism of
Marx and Engels is "absolutely atheistic, and definitely hostile
to *all* religion." He called religion "one of the most corrupt
things existing in the world. . . ." As for Christian socialism, he
called it "the sorriest sort of 'Socialism' and its vilest perversion.
. . ."[2] This blanket condemnation of Christianity has been and
continues to be the position of Soviet orthodoxy. But in order
to establish a point of contact with liberal-minded Christians,
dialogical Marxists have chosen to challenge this condemnation
by reviving the distinction between "good" or heretically chiliastic forms of Christianity (which usually encourage political
radicalism), and "bad" or so-called Constantinian forms of
Christianity (which usually discourage political radicalism), and
by rehabilitating modern Christian socialism.

For the past hundred or more years, Christians have generally
been hostile to Marxism. Leaving aside the question of possible
class prejudice, they have been affronted by Marxist determinism which they saw as a denial of human freedom and spiritu-
ality. They have also perceived that Marxism was intent on blas-
pheming God and destroying religion. With the discussion surrounding the young Marx, some Christians discovered
"another" Marxism and the existence of unusual Marxists. Furthermore, they learned that there are Marxists who seemingly
have no taste for persecuting Christians. These Christians began
to distinguish between a "bad" and presumably obsolete Marxism (Stalinist and neo-Stalinist), and a "good" and promising
Marxism (humanistic and undogmatic). Breaking away from a

liberal anti-Communism that seemed to promote cold war abroad and inhibit radical reform at home, and from a theology that offered no challenge to these conditions, they uncovered a "new" left.

Synthetic Marxist-Christian dialogue rests on such distinctions between "good" and "bad" forms of Christianity and Marxism. Synthetic dialogue requires, quite simply, that the "good" Christians repudiate "bad" Christianity, and that the "good" Marxists repudiate "bad" Marxism. These are painless repudiations because there is widespread agreement among dialogical Marxists and Christians that when Christians give up "Constantinian" Christianity and affirm heretical chiliasm they are giving up a counterfeit and rediscovering the genuine article. Likewise, it is felt that when Marxists relinquish "Stalinistic" (increasingly a euphemism for "Soviet") Marxism and adopt a humanistic Marxism, they are discarding a perversion and reclaiming the authentic meaning of Marxism. This is not to say that orthodox Christianity must be precisely "Constantinian" (since Constantinian Christianity is but one expression of orthodoxy) or that orthodox Marxism must be exactly "Stalinistic" (since Stalinism is but one expression of orthodox Marxism). It is simply that attacks on orthodox Christianity are often construed as attacks on Constantinian Christianity and attacks on orthodox Marxism are often cast as attacks on Stalinism.

According to Leslie Dewart, a substantive or synthetic dialogue presupposes a theory of "doctrinal development," that is, doctrinal innovation and revision. What Dewart has in mind is a "deepening" of one's doctrinal tradition all the while remaining "faithful" to that tradition.[3] Obviously, everything hangs on what is meant by "deepening" and "faithful," what one regards as the essence of Marxism or Christianity. Dewart, for one, sees the essence of Christianity in "the truth of Communism," which is "a Christian truth betrayed by the Church of Christian believers and kept alive by the Church of Christian unbelievers through schism, heresy and apostasy."[4] Garaudy echoes Dewart by saying that a Marxist-Christian convergence will be facilitated "if a Catholic is a better Catholic, and a Marxist a better Marxist. . . ."[5] The assumption here is that when encrustations, distortions, and irrelevancies are peeled away it will be revealed that the essences of Christianity and Marxism are remarkably similar and eminently compatible. We have already seen what Garaudy regards as the "essences" of Christianity and Marxism.

We have argued above that dialogical Christianity and dialogical Marxism are certainly compatible, and that a Marxist-Christian convergence certainly does require "doctrinal development"—and that of a very special kind, namely, heresy and revisionism. Indeed, *this* doctrinal development is entirely inimical to the doctrinal development that forms the basis of the orthodox traditions in Marxism and Christianity.

The Marxist-Christian convergence or alliance has developed to such a point that dialogical Christians and dialogical Marxists are finding it increasingly difficult to communicate with the traditionalists of their own persuasion. Moltmann himself said: "Nowadays you often find yourself in more accord with the reformers in the other camp than with the conservatives in your own."[6] Not surprisingly, the more that dissident Marxists and dissident Christians talked with each other, the more they discovered—to their delight—how much they had in common—to the point of forming a de facto alliance. Moltmann summarized the situation well:

> those involved in Christian-Marxist conversation have been pleased to describe the inner dialectic of Christianity as a conflict between a Constantinian, conservative, state church kind of Christianity and a chiliastic, critical-heretical kind. On the other hand, by virtual analogy they have learned to distinguish between a Stalinistic Marxism (with the Byzantine characteristics of a state

ideology and a conservative practice) and a critical, humanistic Marxism. These mutual self-distinctions are very helpful. They indicate that today the front in the struggle for freedom from humiliation runs down the middle of both movements, and the nonconformists from both camps recognize each other as possible partners in a new alliance.[7]

According to the dialogical American Catholic, Rosemary Ruether, liberals and traditionalists in the Catholic Church "seldom if ever really come into any kind of dialogue, and when they are forced into a confrontation . . . the result turns out to be double monologues which lack even the most elementary consensus that would make real communication possible."[8] This failure to communicate is symptomatic of the gulf separating dialogical and nondialogical Christianity, and would seem to indicate that the future of liberal or dialogical Christianity within the Catholic Church is precarious.

Significantly, there is an analogous failure of communication between revisionists and institutional Marxists in several countries where revisionism had previously enjoyed a certain freedom of expression. In both Eastern and Western Europe dialogical Marxists (as well as revisionists in general) are under great pressure. In France, Garaudy was expelled from the Party. Gilbert Mury quit the Party to join up with the French Maoists. In Germany, Ernst Bloch fled the East to seek asylum in the West where he remains in disgrace in the eyes of the East German Party. In Poland, Leszek Kolakowski was expelled from the Party and now lives in exile. In Czechoslovakia, Milan Machovec went into exile, Vitezslav Gardavsky was expelled from the Party, and Erika Kadlecova lives in disgrace. In many, but not all cases the Soviet invasion of Czechoslovakia was the moment of truth. Only in Italy, Spain, Great Britain, and Yugoslavia have dialogical Communists enjoyed encouragement. It is one of the enduring ironies of the dialogue that many of those Marxists who have paid enough serious attention to Christianity to be able to cultivate its heterodox tendencies have found themselves anathematized as heretics by their own comrades. Such are the fruits of lusting after strange gods.

But the greatest irony of the Marxist-Christian dialogue is that as it has advanced it has become more and more monological and less and less dialogical. What began as a momentous conversation between two great belief systems has proceeded to become a monologue based on the dismemberment of both. Dialogical Christians and dialogical Marxists came to hold so many views in common that, in the words of Alvin C. Currier (himself a dialogical Christian), "separation into the categories of Christian and Marxist seemed inconsequential."[9]

I have had to conclude that Marxism and Christianity are disjunctive belief systems that cannot be fused without doing violence to the integrity of both. This conclusion, I hope, will have been conceptually therapeutic, will have clearly demonstrated the issues at hand. The reader should now be aware of the price to be paid for Marxist-Christian convergence; but it is ultimately up to him or her to determine whether it is a price worth paying. I hope that those Marxists and Christians who have been disturbed by this conclusion will feel encouraged, even stimulated, to think anew about what they believe and why.

Although the conclusions of this study have been overwhelmingly critical in character, there is no reason why we must end on a negative, aloof, or impersonally academic note. Allow me a few personal comments from a Christian viewpoint.

There is a great deal that can be said about Marxist-Christian dialogue which is affirmative in character. It is, no doubt, desirable that Marxists and Christians should talk to one another rather than kill one another. Moreover, no great harm is done to Christianity if Christians collaborate with Marxists in the building of a better society—so long as the Christians are under no illusions that they are engaged in salvific or redemptive activity, so long as they respect the liberty of other Christians to come to different political conclusions, so long as they do not turn Marxist claims into articles of the Christian faith, and so long as they can be reasonably sure that a government led by Marxists will not persecute Christians or eradicate Christian values.

Marxists and Christians *can* engage in dialogue, they *can* work together—without engaging in dubious synthetic ventures. But however dubious those ventures are, it must be conceded that they are the products of genuinely good will, not ill will. That is perhaps why synthetic dialogue has received so little criticism—and, indeed, why I feel a bit like a mischievous rogue for having written this book. After all, to want to turn a fallen world into a New Jerusalem is not, on the face of it, a despicable desire. Indeed, it is a noble aspiration! Those Marxists and dialogical Christians who labor for an earthly New Jerusalem are surely *good* people—but they are good to a fault! From the orthodox point of view—which is also my point of view—these modern Gnostics do not sin out of a perverse craving for carnality, turpitude, or evil. If anything, they sin out of a virtuous impatience, out of a restless hunger for another world, out of a sincere desire for perfection. In effect they desire to be as gods—just as Adam and Eve did. This is a curious sin, for is not imitation the sincerest form of flattery? How strange that God should be offended by his children's effusive imitation.

It often seems bizarre that Christians are expected to accept their creatureliness rather than flee from it, to accept the order of creation instead of taking flight from it. But Christians are instructed that creation is good though flawed; it is God's gift, to be received with patience, with forbearance, and even—if possible—with joy. The martyr, Dietrich Bonhoeffer, expressed this outlook in classic terms:

for a man in his wife's arms to be hankering after the other world
is, in mild terms, a piece of bad taste, and not God's will. We
ought to find and love God in what he actually gives us; if it
pleases him to allow us to enjoy some overwhelming earthly happiness, we must not try to be more pious than God himself and
allow our happiness to be corrupted by presumption and arrogance, and by unbridled religious fantasy which is never satisfied
with what God gives. God will see to it that the man who finds
him in his earthly happiness and thanks him for it does not lack
reminder that earthly things are transient . . . and that sooner or
later there will be times when he can say in all sincerity, "I wish I
were home." But everything has its time, and the main thing is
that we keep step with God. . . . It is presumptuous to want to
have everything at once—matrimonial bliss, the cross, and the
heavenly Jerusalem. . . . [10]

Yes, the New Jerusalem will come—but in God's good time. In
the meantime, Christians are expected to keep pace with God.
Those who lack patience with God's sovereign Providence, who
think themselves more pious than God himself, who want to
leap out of their creaturely condition before the appointed
time—they will ultimately come to call themselves, correctly,
"atheists." The sin of messianic atheism, it seems, is like so
many sins—beautiful, honorable, and very tempting!

Pity the orthodox, for, alas, what they must defend—this present world, this frail body, this life so very full of ugliness—is, as
they supremely know, a lost cause.

NOTES

1. Karl Marx and Friedrich Engels, "Manifesto of the Communist Party," *Marx and Engels: Basic Writings on Politics and Philosophy,*
   Lewis S. Feuer, ed. (Garden City, N.Y.: Anchor, 1959), p. 31.
2. Lenin, *Religion* (New York: International, 1969), pp. 11, 37–38, 45.
   Italics added.
3. Leslie Dewart, "Introduction—From Dialogue to Cooperation,"
   AD, pp. 14–17.

4. Dewart, in *Spectrum of Catholic Attitudes,* Robert Campbell, O.P., ed. (Milwaukee: Bruce, 1969), p. 157.

5. Quoted in Dewart, "Introduction—From Dialogue to Cooperation," *AD,* p. 20.

6. Moltmann, "Politics and the Practice of Hope," *TCC, LXXXVII* (March 11, 1970), p. 290.

7. Moltmann, "Die Revolution der Freiheit," *Perspektiven der Theologie: Gesammelte Aufsaetze* (Munich: Kaiser, and Mainz: Matthias-Gruenewald, 1968), p. 198 (the translation is mine). A shorter and somewhat different version of this essay was delivered by Moltmann as a speech and translated into English in *RRF,* pp. 63–82. The quotation from the German edition is more explicit than the parallel selection in the English version (where the word "heretical" is omitted).

8. Rosemary Ruether, "The Free Church Movement in Contemporary Catholicism," *New Theology No. 6,* Martin E. Marty and Dean G. Peerman, eds. (New York: Macmillan, 1969), pp. 272–273.

9. Alvin C. Currier, "The Caterpillar of Christian-Marxist Dialogue and the Butterfly of the New Consciousness," *TCC, XCI* (March 27, 1974), p. 348.

10. Dietrich Bonhoeffer, *Letters and Papers from Prison,* rev. ed. (New York: Macmillan, 1967), p. 94.

Selected Bibliography

Althusser, Louis, *For Marx* (New York: Vintage, 1969).

Altizer, Thomas J. J., "The Challenge of Modern Gnosticism," *The Journal of Bible and Religion, XXX* (January 1962), pp. 18–25.

Alves, Rubém A., *A Theology of Human Hope* (foreword by Harvey Cox) (St. Meinrad, Ind.: Abbey, 1971).

American Behavioral Scientist, 16 (November-December 1972), special issue on "Millenarian Change: Movements of Total Transformation."

Andras, Charles, "The Christian-Marxist Dialogue," *East Europe, 17* (March 1968), pp. 11–16.

Aptheker, Herbert, *The Urgency of Marxist-Christian Dialogue* (New York: Harper & Row, 1970).

———, ed., *Marxism and Christianity* (New York: Humanities Press, 1968).

Avineri, Shlomo, *The Social and Political Thought of Karl Marx* (Cambridge: Cambridge University Press, 1968).

——, ed., *Marx's Socialism* (New York: Lieber-Atherton, 1973).

Ballard, Paul H., "Harvey Cox: A Theology of Style," *The Reformed World* (Geneva), *32* (June 1972), pp. 51–62.

Barth, Karl, *Against the Stream* (London: SCM Press, 1954).

——, *The German Church Conflict* (Richmond: John Knox, 1965).

——, and Johannes Hamel, *How to Serve God in a Marxist Land* (New York: Association, 1959).

"Barth to Bereczky: A Letter," *The Christian Century, LXIX* (July 30, 1952), pp. 876–877.

Baum, Gregory, ed., *The Future of Belief Debate* (New York: Herder and Herder, 1967).

Benz, Ernst, *Ecclesia Spiritualis* (Stuttgart: Kohlhammer, 1934).

——, *Evolution and Christian Hope* (Garden City, N.Y.: Anchor, 1966).

Berger, Peter L., "A Call for Authority in the Christian Community," *The Princeton Seminary Bulletin, 64* (December 1971), pp. 14–24.

——, *A Rumor of Angels* (Garden City, N.Y.: Doubleday, 1969).

——, et al., "An Appeal for Theological Affirmation" (known as "The Hartford Appeal"), *Worldview, 18* (April 1975), pp. 39–41.

Bigo, Pierre, *Marxisme et Humanisme* (Paris: Presses Universitaires de France, 1953, 1961).

Bloch, Ernst, *Man on His Own* (New York: Herder and Herder, 1970).

——, *Thomas Muentzer als Theologe der Revolution* (Berlin: Aufbau Verlag, 1962).

——, *Das Prinzip Hoffnung,* 2 vols. (Frankfurt a. M.: Suhrkamp, 1959).

Bochenski, I. M., "Soviet-Christian Dialog?" *Listening, III* (1968), pp. 68–75.

Bochenski, J. M., *Soviet Russian Dialectical Materialism* (Dordrecht: D. Reidel, 1963).

Callahan, Daniel, ed., *The Secular City Debate* (New York: Macmillan, 1966).

Calvez, Jean-Yves, *La Pensée de Karl Marx* (Paris: Editions du Seuil, 1956).

Caporale, Rocco, and Antonio Grumelli, eds., *The Culture of Unbelief* (Berkeley: University of California Press, 1971).

Capps, Walter H., *Time Invades the Cathedral: Tensions in the School of Hope* (Philadelphia: Fortress, 1972).

———, ed., *The Future of Hope* (Philadelphia: Fortress, 1970).

Charles, R. H., *Eschatology* (New York: Schocken, 1963).

Clasen, Claus-Peter, *Anabaptism: A Social History, 1525–1618: Switzerland, Austria, Moravia, South and Central Germany* (Ithaca, N.Y.: Cornell University Press, 1972).

Cohn, Norman, *The Pursuit of the Millennium* (New York: Harper & Row, 1961). Rev. Ed.: (New York: Oxford University Press, 1970).

Coser, Lewis A., "The Militant Collective: Jesuits and Leninists," *Social Research, 40* (Spring 1973), pp. 110–128.

———, "Millenarians, Totalitarians and Utopians," *Dissent, V* (Winter 1958), pp. 67–72.

Cottier, Georges M.-M., *L'Athéisme du jeune Marx: Ses origines hégéliennes* (Paris: Librairie philosophique J. Vrin, 1959).

———, *Chrétiens et marxistes: Dialogue avec Roger Garaudy* (Tours: Mame, 1967).

Cousins, Ewert H., ed., *Hope and the Future of Man* (Philadelphia: Fortress, 1972).

Cox, Harvey G., "The Biblical Basis of the Geneva Conference," *The Christian Century, LXXXIV* (April 5, 1967), pp. 435–437.

———, "The Churches and the Future of Religion," *Christianity and Crisis, 33* (February 5, 1973), pp. 9–11.

———, "Discussion: Communist-Christian Dialogue," *Union Seminary Quarterly Review, XXII* (March 1967), pp. 223–227.

———, "Feasibility and Fantasy: Sources of Social Transcendence," *The Religious Situation 1969*, Donald R. Cutler, ed. (Boston: Beacon, 1969), pp. 910–920.

———, *The Feast of Fools* (New York: Harper & Row, 1969).

———, *God's Revolution and Man's Responsibility* (Valley Forge, Pa.: Judson, 1965).

———, "I Am for Kennedy," *Christianity and Crisis, XXVIII* (June 10, 1968), pp. 132–133.

———, "Marxist Humanism in Eastern Europe—Problems and Prospects," *The Correspondent,* No. 33 (Winter 1965), pp. 30–44.

———, "The New Christian Soldiers: Ferment in the Churches," *The Nation, 201* (October 11, 1965), pp. 216–220.

———, "No Christological Center" (from "The Harford Appeal: A Symposium"), *Worldview, 18* (May 1975), pp. 22–23.

———, "Non-Theistic Commitment," *Cross Currents, XIX* (Fall 1969), pp. 400–407.

———, *On Not Leaving It to the Snake* (New York: Macmillan, 1967) (essays).

———, "Political Theology for the United States," *Projections: Shaping an American Theology for the Future,* Thomas F. O'Meara and Donald M. Weisser, eds. (Garden City, N.Y.: Image, 1970), pp. 49–57.

———, "Religion in the Age of Aquarius" (conversation with T. George Harris), *Psychology Today, 3* (April 1970), pp. 45, 47, 62–64, 66–67.

———, *The Secular City,* rev. ed. (New York: Macmillan, 1966).

———, "'The Secular City'—Ten Years Later," *The Christian Century, XCII* (May 28, 1975), pp. 544–547.

———, "The Secular Search for Religious Experience," *Theology Today, XXV* (October 1968), pp. 320–332.

———, *The Seduction of the Spirit* (New York: Simon and Schuster, 1973).

———, "Technology, Modern Man, and the Gospel" (panel discussion with Carl F. H. Henry), *Christianity Today, XII* (July 5, 1968), pp. 3–7.

———, "A Theological Travel Diary: East Germany and Czechoslovakia, June 1963," *Andover Newton Quarterly, 4* (November 1963), pp. 26–36.

————, "Tired Images Transcended: An Interview with Myself," *The Christian Century, LXXXVII* (April 1, 1970), pp. 384–386.

————, "Using and Misusing Bonhoeffer," *Christianity and Crisis, XXIV* (October 19, 1964), pp. 199–201.

————, ed., *The Church Amid Revolution* (New York: Association, 1967).

Cranston, Maurice, "The Thought of Roger Garaudy," *Problems of Communism, XIX* (September-October 1970), pp. 11–18.

Cuénot, Claude (with a comment by Roger Garaudy), *Science and Faith in Teilhard de Chardin* (London: Garnstone, 1967).

Cullmann, Oscar, *Jesus and the Revolutionaries* (New York: Harper & Row, 1970).

————, *The State in the New Testament* (New York: Scribner's, 1956).

Cunningham, Adrian, et al., *Catholics and the Left* (Springfield, Ill.: Templegate, 1966).

Danielou, Jean, *Prayer as a Political Problem* (New York: Sheed and Ward, 1967).

D'Arcy, Martin, *Communism and Christianity* (Great Britain: Penguin, 1956).

Dean, Thomas, *Post-Theistic Thinking: The Marxist-Christian Dialogue in Radical Perspective* (Philadelphia: Temple University Press, 1975).

DeGeorge, Richard T., *The New Marxism* (New York: Pegasus, 1968).

————, *Patterns of Soviet Thought* (Ann Arbor: University of Michigan Press, 1966).

————, *Soviet Ethics and Morality* (Ann Arbor: University of Michigan Press, 1969).

Delfgaauw, Bernard, *The Young Marx* (Westminster, Md.: Newman, 1967).

de Lubac, S. J., Henri, *The Drama of Atheist Humanism* (Cleveland: Meridian, 1963).

Demaitre, Edmund, "The Christian-Marxist Dialogue," *Communist Af-*

fairs, 5 (July-August 1967), pp. 3–8.

———, "An Inconclusive Dialogue," *Problems of Communism, XX* (September-October 1971), pp. 41–47.

Devlin, Kevin, "The Catholic-Communist 'Dialogue,'" *Problems of Communism, XV* (May-June 1966), pp. 31–38.

Dewart, Leslie, "Christians and Marxians in Dialogue," *Continuum, I* (Summer 1963), pp. 139–153.

———, *The Foundations of Belief* (New York: Herder and Herder, 1969).

———, *The Future of Belief* (New York: Herder and Herder, 1966).

Domenach, Jean-Marie, and Robert Montvalon, *The Catholic Avant-Garde* (New York: Holt, Rinehart and Winston, 1967).

Ello, Paul, ed., *Czechoslovakia's Blueprint for "Freedom"* (Washington, D.C.: Acropolis Books, 1968).

Ellul, Jacques, *False Presence of the Kingdom* (New York: Seabury, 1972).

———, *The Meaning of the City* (Grand Rapids: Eerdmans, 1970).

———, *The Presence of the Kingdom* (New York: Seabury, 1967).

Engels, Frederick, *The Peasant War in Germany* (New York: International, 1926).

Fetscher, Iring, *Marx and Marxism* (New York: Herder and Herder, 1971).

Feuer, Lewis S., *Marx and the Intellectuals* (Garden City, N.Y.: Anchor, 1969).

———, ed., *Marx and Engels: Basic Writings on Politics and Philosophy* (Garden City, N.Y.: Anchor, 1959).

Feuerbach, Ludwig, *The Essence of Christianity* (New York: Harper & Row, 1957).

———, *The Essence of Faith According to Luther* (New York: Harper & Row, 1967).

———, *Lectures on the Essence of Religion* (New York: Harper & Row, 1967).

Fiorenza, Francis P., "Dialectical Theology and Hope, I," *Heythrop Journal, 9* (1968), pp. 143–163.

———, "Dialectical Theology and Hope, II," *Heythrop Journal, 9* (1968), pp. 384–399.

———, "Dialectical Theology and Hope, III" *Heythrop Journal, 10* (1969), pp. 26–42.

Fitch, Robert E., "The Protestant Sickness," *Religion in Life, XXXV* (Autumn 1966), pp. 498–503.

———, "The Sell-Out or The Well Acculturated Christian," *The Christian Century, LXXXIII* (February 16, 1966), pp. 202–205.

Fitzsimons, M. A., "The Role of Providence in History," *The Review of Politics, 35* (July 1973), pp. 386–397.

Franz, Guenther, ed., *Thomas Muentzer: Schriften und Briefe* (Guetersloh: Gerd Mohn, 1968).

Friesen, Abraham, *Reformation and Utopia: The Marxist Interpretations of the Reformation and Its Antecedents* (Wiesbaden, West Germany: Franz Steiner, 1974).

Fromm, Erich, *Marx's Concept of Man* (New York: Ungar, 1961).

———, ed., *Socialist Humanism* (Garden City, N.Y.: Anchor, 1965).

Garaudy, Roger, *The Alternative Future: A Vision of Christian Marxism* (New York: Simon and Schuster, 1974).

———, "Communistes et Catholiques: Apres l'encyclique 'Pacem in Terris,'" supplement to *Cahiers du Communisme,* No. 7–8 (July-August 1963), pp. 1–23.

———, "Communists and Christians in Dialogue," *Union Seminary Quarterly Review, XXII* (March 1967), pp. 205–212.

———, *The Crisis in Communism* (New York: Grove, 1970).

———, *Dieu est mort (étude sur Hegel)* (Paris: Presses Universitaires de France, 1962).

———, *L'Église, le communisme et les chrétiens* (Paris: Editions Sociales, 1949).

———, "Faith and Revolution," *Cross Currents, XXIII* (Spring 1973), pp. 31–47.

————, *From Anathema to Dialogue* (New York: Vintage, 1966).

————, *Karl Marx: The Evolution of His Thought* (New York: International, 1967).

————, *Lénine* (Paris: Presses Universitaires de France, 1968).

————, *Marxism in the Twentieth Century* (New York: Scribner's, 1970).

————, "New Goals for Socialism," *The Center Magazine, V* (September-October 1972), pp. 33–37.

————, *Perspectives de l'homme: Existentialisme, pensée catholique, marxisme* (Paris: Presses Universitaires de France, 1962).

————, *Peut-on être communiste aujourd'hui?* (Paris: Grasset, 1968). (This book was revised and reissued after the May 1968 crisis in France and the Soviet invasion of Czechoslovakia as *Pour un modèle français du socialisme*.

————, *Pour un modèle français du socialisme* (Paris: Gallimard, 1968).

————, *Le problème chinois* (Paris: Seghers, 1967).

————, *Reconquête de l'espoir* (Paris: Grasset, 1971).

————, "We are Struggling on Behalf of Man," *Political Affairs, XLV* (July 1966), pp. 18–24.

————, "What Does a Non-Christian Expect of the Church in Matters of Social Morality?" *The Social Message of the Gospels,* Franz Boeckle, ed. (New York: Paulist, 1968), pp. 24–45.

————, *The Whole Truth* (London: Fontana/Collins, 1971).

————, ed., *La Liberté en sursis—Prague 1968* (Paris: Fayard, 1968) (Garaudy's "Introduction" is translated in Garaudy, *The Whole Truth,* pp. 64–81.)

————, and Quentin Lauer, S.J., *A Christian-Communist Dialogue* (Garden City, N.Y.: Doubleday, 1968).

————, et al., "Initiative in History: A Christian-Marxist Exchange" (pamphlet) (Cambridge, Mass.: The Church Society for College Work, 1967).

Girardi, Giulio, *Marxism and Christianity* (New York: Macmillan, 1968).

Glayman, Claude, ed., *Garaudy par Garaudy* (Paris: La Table Ronde, 1970).

Golan, Galia, *Reform Rule in Czechoslovakia* (London: Cambridge University Press, 1973).

Gollwitzer, Helmut, *The Christian Faith and the Marxist Criticism of Religion* (New York: Scribner's, 1970).

———, *The Demands of Freedom* (New York: Harper & Row, 1965).

Grant, Robert M., *Gnosticism and Early Christianity*, rev. ed. (New York: Harper & Row, 1966).

Gregor, A. James, "Marxism and Ethics: A Methodological Inquiry," *Philosophy and Phenomenological Research, XXVIII* (March 1968), pp. 368–384.

———, *A Survey of Marxism* (New York: Random House, 1965).

Gritsch, Eric W., *Reformer Without a Church: The Life and Thought of Thomas Muentzer: 1488 [?]–1525* (Philadelphia: Fortress, 1967).

Guitton, Jean, *Great Heresies and Church Councils* (New York: Harper & Row, 1965).

Gutiérrez, Gustavo, *A Theology of Liberation* (Maryknoll, N.Y.: Orbis, 1973).

Hall, Douglas J., "The Theology of Hope in an Officially Optimistic Society," *Religion in Life, XL* (Autumn 1971), pp. 376–390.

Harrington, Michael, "Marx versus Marx," *New Politics, 1* (Fall 1961), pp. 112–123.

Herzog, Frederick, ed., *The Future of Hope* (New York: Herder and Herder, 1970).

Heschel, Abraham J., *The Prophets,* 2 Vols. (New York: Harper & Row, 1962).

Hitchcock, James, *The Decline and Fall of Radical Catholicism* (New York: Herder and Herder, 1971).

Hook, Sidney, *From Hegel to Marx* (Ann Arbor: University of Michigan Press, 1962).

————, "Marx's Second Coming," *Problems of Communism, XV* (July–August 1966), pp. 26–29.

Hordern, William, *Christianity, Communism and History* (New York: Abingdon, 1954).

Janos, Andrew C., "The Communist Theory of the State and Revolution," *Communism and Revolution,* Cyril E. Black and Thomas P. Thornton, eds. (Princeton: Princeton University Press, 1964), pp. 27–41.

Jonas, Hans, *The Gnostic Religion,* rev. ed. (Boston: Beacon, 1963).

Jordan, Z. A., *The Evolution of Dialectical Materialism* (New York: St. Martin's, 1967).

Kamenka, Eugene, *The Ethical Foundations of Marxism* (New York: Praeger, 1962).

Kellner, Erich, ed., *Christentum und Marxismus Heute* (Vienna: Europa Verlag, 1966).

————, ed., *Schoepfertum und Freiheit in einer humanen Gesellschaft; Marienbader Protokolle* (Vienna: Europa Verlag, 1969).

Klugmann, James, ed., *Dialogue of Christianity and Marxism* (London: Lawrence and Wishart, 1966).

Knox, R. A., *Enthusiasm* (Oxford: Oxford University Press, 1950).

Kuemmel, W. G., *Promise and Fulfillment: The Eschatological Message of Jesus* (London: SCM Press, 1957).

Kusin, Vladimir V., *The Intellectual Origins of the Prague Spring* (London: Cambridge University Press, 1971).

————, *Political Grouping in the Czechoslovak Reform Movement* (New York: Columbia University Press, 1972).

Labedz, Leopold, ed., *Revisionism* (New York: Praeger, 1962.).

Ladd, George Eldon, *The Presence of the Future* (Grand Rapids: Eerdmans, 1974).

Lauer, S. J., Quentin, "Christian-Marxist Dialogue: An Evaluation," *Worldview, 14* (March 1971), pp. 15–19.

Lebreton, S.J., Jacques, and Jacques Zeiller, *Heresy and Orthodoxy* (New York: Collier, 1946).

Leff, Gordon, *Heresy in the Later Middle Ages: The Relation of Heterodoxy to Dissent, c. 1250—c. 1450,* 2 vols. (New York: Barnes & Noble, 1967).

Lenin, V. I., *Imperialism: The Highest Stage of Capitalism* (New York: International, 1969).

————, *Religion* (New York: International, 1933).

————, "Socialism and Religion" (pamphlet) (Moscow: Progress Publishers, 1968).

————, *What Is to Be Done?* (New York: International, 1969).

Leonhard, Wolfgang, *Three Faces of Marxism* (New York: Holt, Rinehart and Winston, 1974).

Lewy, Guenter, *Religion and Revolution* (New York: Oxford University Press, 1974).

Lichtheim, George, "Czechoslovakia 1968," *Commentary, 46* (November 1968), pp. 63–72.

————, *From Marx to Hegel* (New York: Herder and Herder, 1971).

————, *Marxism* (New York: Praeger, 1962).

————, *Marxism in Modern France* (New York: Columbia University Press, 1966).

Lindblom, Johannes, *Prophecy in Ancient Israel* (Philadelphia: Muhlenberg, 1962).

Littell, Franklin H., *The Origins of Sectarian Protestantism* (New York: Macmillan, 1952).

Lobkowicz, Nicholas, ed., *Marx and the Western World* (Notre Dame, Ind.: University of Notre Dame Press, 1967).

Lochman, Jan Milič, *Church in a Marxist Society* (New York: Harper & Row, 1970).

Loewith, Karl, *Meaning in History* (Chicago: University of Chicago Press, 1949).

Ludz, Peter, "The 'New Socialism': Philosophy in Search of Reality," *Problems of Communism, XVIII* (July–October 1969), pp. 33–42.

Machovec, Milan, *Marxismus und dialektische Theologie* (Zurich: EVZ-Verlag, 1965).

McInnes, Neil, "The Christian-Marxist Dialogue: International Implications," *Survey*, No. 67 (April 1968), pp. 57–76.

————, *The Western Marxists* (New York: Library Press, 1972).

MacIntyre, Alasdair, *Marxism and Christianity*, rev. ed. (New York: Schocken, 1968).

McLellan, David, "Christian-Marxist Dialogue," *New Blackfriars, XLIX,* No. 6 (1968), pp. 462–467.

————, *Karl Marx: His Life and Thought* (New York: Harper & Row, 1973).

————, *Marx Before Marxism* (New York: Harper & Row, 1970).

Macmurray, John, *Creative Society: A Study of the Relation of Christianity to Communism* (New York: Association, 1963).

Mandić, Oleg, "A Marxist Perspective on Contemporary Religious Revivals," *Social Research, 37* (Summer 1970), pp. 237–258.

Marcuse, Herbert, *Reason and Revolution* (New York: Humanities Press, 1954).

————, *Soviet Marxism* (London: Routledge & Kegan Paul, 1958).

————, (with Harvey Wheeler), "Varieties of Humanism," *The Center Magazine, I* (July 1968), pp. 13–15.

Maritain, Jacques, *The Peasant of the Garonne* (New York: Macmillan, 1968).

Marsch, Wolf–Dieter, ed., *Diskussion ueber die "Theologie der Hoffnung" von Juergen Moltmann* (Munich: Kaiser, 1967).

Marty, Martin E., and Dean G. Peerman, eds., *New Theology No. 5* (New York: Macmillan, 1968).

————, *New Theology No. 6* (New York: Macmillan, 1969).

Marx, Karl, *Early Writings,* T. B. Bottomore, ed. (New York: McGraw–Hill, 1964).

————, *Grundrisse: Foundations of the Critique of Political Economy* (New York: Harper & Row, 1971).

————, and Friedrich Engels, *On Religion* (New York: Schocken, 1964).

————, *Selected Works in Two Volumes* (Moscow: Foreign Languages Publishing House, 1962).

Mauriac, François, et al., *Communism and Christians* (London: Paladin, 1938).

Meeks, M. Douglas, *Origins of the Theology of Hope* (Philadelphia: Fortress, 1974).

Metz, Johannes B., ed., *Faith and the World of Politics* (New York: Paulist, 1968).

Meyer, Alfred G., *Leninism* (New York: Praeger, 1957).

Migliore, Daniel L., "Biblical Eschatology and Political Hermeneutics," *Theology Today, XXVI* (July 1969), pp. 116–132.

Mojzes, Paul, "Christian-Marxist Encounter in the Context of a Socialist Society," *Journal of Ecumenical Studies, IX* (Winter 1972), pp. 1–27.

Molnar, Thomas, *God and the Knowledge of Reality* (New York: Basic Books, 1973).

————, "Notes on the Dialogue: Does Dialogue Mean Capitulation?" *Worldview, 9* (January 1966), pp. 4–8.

Moltmann, Juergen, "The Cross and Civil Religion," *Religion and Political Society,* The Institute of Christian Thought, ed. (New York: Harper & Row, 1974), pp. 11–47.

————, *The Crucified God* (New York: Harper & Row, 1974).

————, "Descent into Hell," *Duke Divinity School Review, 33* (Spring 1968), pp. 115–119.

————, "Eternity," *Listening, 3* (1968), pp. 89–95.

————, *The Experiment Hope* (Philadelphia: Fortress, 1975) (essays).

————, "The Future as Threat and as Opportunity," *The Religious Situation 1969,* Donald R. Culter, ed. (Boston: Beacon, 1969), pp. 921–941.

————, *The Gospel of Liberation* (Waco, Texas: Word, 1973) (sermons).

————, *Hope and Planning* (New York: Harper & Row, 1971) (essays).

————, "Hope Beyond Time," *Duke Divinity School Review, 33* (Spring 1968), 109–114.

————, "Hope Without Faith: An Eschatological Humanism Without God," *Is God Dead?*, Johannes B. Metz, ed. (New York: Paulist, 1966), pp. 25–40.

————, "Die Kategorie Novum in der christlichen Theologie," *Ernst Bloch zu ehren: Beitraege zu seinem Werk* (Frankfurt a.M.: Suhrkamp, 1965), pp. 243–263.

————, "The Lordship of Christ and Human Society," *Two Studies in the Theology of Bonhoeffer*, Juergen Moltmann and Juergen Weissbach (New York: Scribner's, 1967), pp. 21–94.

————, *Man* (Philadelphia: Fortress, 1974).

————, "Man and the Son of Man," *No Man Is Alien: Essays on the Unity of Mankind*, J. Robert Nelson, ed. (Leiden: E. J. Brill, 1971), pp. 203–224.

————, "Messianismus und Marxismus," *Ueber Ernst Bloch: Mit Beitraegen von Martin Walser et al.* (Frankfurt a.M.: Suhrkamp, 1968), pp. 42–60.

————, "An Open Letter to José Miguez Bonino: On Latin American Liberation Theology," *Christianity and Crisis, 36* (March 29, 1976), pp. 57–63.

————, *Perspektiven der Theologie: Gesammelte Aufsaetze* (Munich: Kaiser, and Mainz: Matthias-Gruenewald, 1968) (essays).

————, "Politics and the Practice of Hope," *The Christian Century, LXXXVII* (March 11, 1970), pp. 288–291.

————, "The Realism of Hope: The Feast of the Resurrection and the Transformation of the Present Reality," *Concordia Theological Monthly, XL* (March 1969), pp. 149–155.

————, *Religion, Revolution and the Future* (New York: Scribner's, 1969) (essays).

————, *Theology of Hope* (New York: Harper & Row, 1967).

————, *Theology of Play* (New York: Harper & Row, 1972).

————, "The Theology of Revolution," *New Christian* (London), *84* (December 12, 1968), pp. 9–10.

Momjan, H., *Marxism and the Renegade Garaudy* (Moscow: Progress Publishers, 1974).

Moore, Stanley, *Three Tactics: The Background in Marx* (New York: Monthly Review Press, 1963).

Morgenthau, Hans J., "The Fate of Czechoslovakia: Why the Soviet Union Moved In," *The New Republic, 159* (December 7, 1968), pp. 19–21.

Muckenhirn, Maryellen, ed., *The Future as the Presence of Shared Hope* (New York: Sheed and Ward, 1968).

Murchland, Bernard, "Christianity and Communism: The Emerging Dialogue," *Worldview, 12* (November 1969), pp. 12–14.

Neuhaus, Richard J., "Liberation Theology and the Captivities of Jesus," *Worldview, 16* (June 1973), pp. 41–48.

Niebuhr, H. Richard, *Christ and Culture* (New York: Harper & Row, 1951).

———, *The Kingdom of God in America* (New York: Harper & Row, 1937).

Niebuhr, Reinhold, *Beyond Tragedy* (New York: Scribner's, 1965).

———, *The Children of Light and the Children of Darkness* (New York: Scribner's, 1960).

———, *Christian Realism and Political Problems* (New York: Scribner's, 1953).

———, *Essays in Applied Christianity* (New York: Meridian, 1959).

———, *The Nature and Destiny of Man*, 2 Vols. (New York: Scribner's, 1964).

Niggs, Walter, *The Heretics* (New York: Knopf, 1962).

Norris, Russell B., *God, Marx, and the Future: Dialogue with Roger Garaudy* (Philadelphia: Fortress, 1974).

O'Collins, Gerald, *Man and His New Hopes* (New York: Herder and Herder, 1969).

Oestreicher, Paul, ed., *The Christian Marxist Dialogue* (New York: Macmillan, 1969).

Ogletree, Thomas W., ed., *Openings for Marxist-Christian Dialogue* (New York: Abingdon, 1969).

Ollman, Bertell, *Alienation: Marx's Conception of Man in Capitalist Society* (London: Cambridge University Press, 1971).

Ozment, Steven, *Mysticism and Dissent: Religious Ideology and Social Protest in the Sixteenth Century* (New Haven, Conn.: Yale University Press, 1973).

Paolucci, Henry, ed., *The Political Writings of St. Augustine* (Chicago: Gateway, 1962).

Pelikan, Jaroslav, *The Christian Tradition: A History of the Development of Doctrine, Vol. 1: The Emergence of the Catholic Tradition (100–600)* (Chicago: University of Chicago Press, 1971).

Perottino, Serge, *Garaudy* (Paris: Seghers, 1969).

Perrin, Henri, *Priest and Worker* (New York: Holt, Rinehart and Winston, 1964).

Perrin, Norman, *The Kingdom of God in the Teaching of Jesus* (Philadelphia: Westminster, 1963).

Raines, John C., and Thomas Dean, eds., *Marxism and Radical Religion* (Philadelphia: Temple University Press, 1970).

Ramsey, Paul, *Who Speaks for the Church?* (New York: Abingdon, 1967).

Reeves, Marjorie, *The Influence of Prophecy in the Later Middle Ages: A Study in Joachimism* (London: Oxford University Press, 1969).

————, and Beatrice Hirsch–Reich, *The Figurae of Joachim of Fiore* (London: Oxford University Press, 1972).

Rhodes, James M., "Dionysian and Promethean Humanism," *Modern Age, 14* (Spring 1970), pp. 174–189.

Ruether, Rosemary Radford, *The Radical Kingdom: The Western Experience of Messianic Hope* (New York: Harper & Row, 1970).

Schaff, Philip, ed., *The Nicene and Post–Nicene Fathers, Volume V: Saint Augustine: Anti–Pelagian Writings* (Grand Rapids: Eerdmans, 1971).

Schillebeeckx, O.P., Edward, and Boniface Willems, O.P., eds, *The Problem of Eschatology* (New York: Paulist, 1969).

Schroeder, W. W., "The Secular City: A Critique," *Religion in Life, XXXV* (Autumn 1966), pp. 504–512.

Schuller, Peter M., "Karl Marx's Atheism," *Science and Society, XXXIX* (Fall 1975), pp. 331–345.

Schultz, Hans Juergen, *Conversion to the World* (foreword by Harvey Cox) (New York: Scribner's, 1967).

Schwarz, Hans, *On the Way to the Future* (Minneapolis: Augsburg, 1972).

Smirin, M. M., *Die Volksreformation des Thomas Muentzer und der grosse deutsche Bauernkrieg*, 2d rev. ed. (Berlin: Dietz Verlag, 1956).

Steel, Ronald, "Up Against the Wall in Prague," *The New York Review of Books, XI* (September 26, 1968), pp. 13–16.

Stoehr, Martin, ed., *Disputation zwischen Christen und Marxisten* (Munich: Kaiser, 1966).

Stoger, Hermann, "Epilogue to Marienbad," *Survey*, No. 66 (January 1968), pp. 117–125.

Svitak, Ivan, *The Czechoslovak Experiment* (New York: Columbia University Press, 1971).

Taborsky, Edward, "The New Era in Czechoslovakia," *East Europe, 17* (November 1968), pp. 19–29.

Taylor, Charles, "The Ambiguities of Marxist Doctrine," *The Student World, LI* (Second Quarter 1958), pp. 157–166.

Terrill, Ross, "Czechoslovakia's New Course: Will Liberalization Lead to Democratization?" *The New Republic, 158* (May 18, 1968), pp. 19–23.

Thrupp, Sylvia L., ed., *Millennial Dreams in Action: Studies in Revolutionary Religious Movements* (New York: Schocken, 1970).

Tinder, Glenn, "Eschatology and Politics," *The Review of Politics, 27* (July 1965), pp. 311–333.

Tripole, Martin R., "Ecclesiological Developments in Moltmann's Theology of Hope," *Theological Studies, 34* (March 1973), pp. 19–35.

Tucker, Robert C., *The Marxian Revolutionary Idea* (New York: Norton, 1969).

————, *Philosophy and Myth in Karl Marx* (London: Cambridge University Press, 1961).

Tuveson, Ernest Lee, *Millennium and Utopia: A Study in the Background of the Idea of Progress* (Gloucester, Mass.: Peter Smith, 1972).

van der Bent, A. J., "A Decade of Christian-Marxist Dialogue: An Historical, Literary and Bibliographical Survey," *Ateismo E Dialogo: bollettino del segretariato per i non credenti* (Vatican City), *VI* (June 1971), pp. 23–34.

van Leeuwen, Arend T., *Prophecy in a Technocratic Era* (foreword by Harvey Cox) (New York: Scribner's, 1968).

Velen, Victor A., "Why Moscow Fears the Czechs," *The New Leader, LI* (April 26, 1968), pp. 5–7.

Verret, M., *Les marxistes et la religion* (Paris: Editions Sociales, 1961).

Vincent, John J., "Some Hesitations on Hope," *Religion in Life, XL* (Spring 1971), pp. 64–73.

Voegelin, Eric, *From Enlightenment to Revolution* (Durham, N.C.: Duke University Press, 1975).

————, *The New Science of Politics* (Chicago: University of Chicago Press, 1952).

————, *Science, Politics and Gnosticism* (Chicago: Gateway, 1968).

von Rad, Gerhard, *The Message of the Prophets* (London: SCM Press, 1968).

Vree, Dale, "Coalition Politics on the Left in France and Italy," *The Review of Politics, 37* (July 1975), pp. 340–356.

————, "Falling Out from the Dialogue," *Worldview, 17* (December 1974), pp. 48–51.

————, "Reflections on Wittgenstein, Religion, and Politics," *Christian Scholar's Review, III*, No. 2 (1973), pp. 113–133.

————, " 'Stripped Clean': The Berrigans and the Politics of Guilt and Martyrdom," *Ethics, 85* (July 1975), pp. 271–287.

————, review of *The Experiment Hope* by J. Moltmann, *Cross Currents, XXV* (Fall 1975), pp. 316–319.

————, review of *Man* by J. Moltmann, *The Crucified God* by J. Moltmann, and *Religion and Political Society* by J. Moltmann et al., *Commonweal, CII* (November 7, 1975), pp. 536–538.

Vulgamore, Melvin L., "The Social Gospel Old and New: Walter Rauschenbusch and Harvey Cox," *Religion in Life, XXXVI* (Winter 1967), pp. 516–533.

Ward, Hiley H., *God and Marx Today* (Philadelphia: Fortress, 1968).

West, Charles C., *Communism and the Theologians* (New York: Macmillan, 1958).

Wetter, S.J., Gustav A., *Dialectical Materialism* (New York: Praeger, 1958).

Wilburn, Ralph G., "Some Questions on Moltmann's Theology of Hope," *Religion in Life, XXXVIII* (Winter 1969), pp. 578–595.

Will, James E., "The Uses of Philosophical Theology in the Christian-Marxist Dialogue," *Union Seminary Quarterly Review, XXVI* (Fall 1970), pp. 19–42.

Williams, George H., *The Radical Reformation* (Philadelphia: Westminster, 1957).

————, and Angel M. Mergal, eds., *Spiritual and Anabaptist Writers* (Philadelphia: Westminster, 1957).

Windsor, Philip, and Adam Roberts, *Czechoslovakia 1968: Reform, Repression and Resistance* (New York: Columbia University Press, 1969).

Yoder, John H., "Exodus and Exile: The Two Faces of Liberation," *Cross Currents, XXIII* (Fall 1973), pp. 297–309.

Zartman, I. William, ed., *Czechoslovakia: Intervention and Impact* (New York: New York University Press, 1970).

Zuck, Lowell H., ed., *Christianity and Revolution: Radical Christian Testimonies, 1520–1650* (Philadelphia: Temple University Press, 1975).

Index